F-102
DELTA DAGGER IN EUROPE

By J.D. Ragay
Illustrated by Perry Manley

squadron/signal publications

If you have any photographs of the aircraft, armor, soldiers or ships of any nation, particularly wartime snapshots, why not share them with us and help make Squadron/Signal's books all the more interesting and complete in the future. Any photograph sent to us will be copied and the original returned. The donor will be fully credited for any photos used. Please send them to:

Squadron/Signal Publications, Inc.
1115 Crowley Drive.
Carrollton, TX 75011-5010.

Dedication

To the F-102 — The Cadillac of Jets

The above description of the F-102 was noted during an interview with CAPT Michael L. Clarke, a pilot with the 32nd TFS who just transitioned from the F-102 to the F-4. Also, in this interview, the Deputy Commander for operations of the 32nd TFS, MAJ Edward F. Mullins stated:

The Deuce was nice to fly and it was a good weapons system. Its passing will not go unnoticed by the many pilots who grew up with the aircraft.

Acknowledgements

This book is the end result of some twenty years of collecting every scrap of information related to the F-102 in Europe. During the period of 1960-69, F-102s were based at Soesterberg Air Base, where the author visited frequently to collect photographs and information.

As part of the research for this book a number of official archives assisted the author with photographs, important documents and unit histories. These include the following: H.Q. USAF Historical Research Center, Maxwell AFB, Alabama; H.Q. USAF Inspection & Safety Center, Norton AFB, California; and the H.Q. USAF Logistics Command, Wright-Patterson AFB, Ohio.

This book also came about as a result of the kind cooperation of many persons over the past twenty years. The author is indebted to them all. It is impossible to name all these people involved. The following, however, deserve special recognition: LTCOL William H. Greenhalgh (USAF, Ret.) who copied hundreds of individual aircraft histories at the USAF Historical Research Center, as well as many other documents.

I am also indebted to MSGT Vernon L. Briley, Squadron Historian of the 32nd TFS; Mr. John F. Vadas, former crew-chief with the 32nd FIS; MAJ Raymond D. Roberts (USAF, Ret.), a former F-102 pilot with the 525th FIS; and Mr. Stephen Chianese, former F-102 crew chief with the 431st FIS. Additionally, thanks must also go to the American Aviation Historical Society, which gave me a F-102 Research Project during 1972, and supported me with numerous contacts.

Contributors

Royal Netherlands AF History Office/Adjudant J. Vanden Berg
36th TFW/CAPT Herbert G. Baker
    CAPT Margaret C. Durrett
50th TFW/SSGT Beatrice A. Liu
316th Air Division/SMSGT Eddie Lee
16th Air Force/Mr. Robert L. Swetzler
Aerospatiale/Mr. J.M. Coudre
AIRSCOOP, HQ USAF Europe/Mr. Bob Howard
Stars and Stripes European Edition/Mrs. Dawn Hutto
LTCOL Barry L. Ream
COL Leslie J. Prichard
COL Dan P. Berry
SSGT Niel L. White
MAJ Win C. Van Breda
COL Wilhelm Goebel
David W. Menard
Larry Davis

Introduction

The Convair F-102 Delta Dagger served in Europe from 28 January 1959 until 16 April 1970. The following six Fighter Interceptor Squadrons (FIS) flew the Delta Dagger in Europe under the command of U.S. Air Force Europe (USAFE), headquartered at Ramstein Air Base, Germany: 32nd FIS based at Soesterberg AB, Netherlands; 431st FIS based at Zaragoza AB, Spain; 496th FIS Hahn AB, Germany; 497th FIS located at Torrejon AB, Spain; 525th FIS at Bitburg AB, Germany; and the 526th FIS at Ramstein AB, Germany.

Missions for USAFE controlled units were directed by the U.S. Air Force Chief of Staff from Washington, D.C. Since USAFE unit would be committed to the North Atlantic Treaty Organization (NATO) in time of war, USAFE NATO missions come under the direction of the Supreme Allied Commander, Supreme Headquarters Allied Powers Europe (SHAPE). Thus, the F-102 units came under a dual command structure.

Under NATO, the Allied Air Forces Central Europe (AAFCE) was divided into the 2nd Allied Tactical Air Force (2 ATAF) and the 4th ATAF, commanded by the Allied Forces Central Europe (AFCENT), although Spanish based units were not part of AFCENT.

As part of this overall structure, the 17th Air Force, at Ramstein AB (within the 4th ATAF) commanded USAF NATO committed units, directing the operations of strike, air defense and reconnaissance units based in France, The Netherlands, Germany, Libya and Italy. This was a mixed force of surface-to-surface missiles (Martin Mace) and supersonic aircraft including the F-100D, RF-101C, F-102A, F-105D and RF-4C.

The Spanish based units came under the command of the 65th Air Division (Defense) at Torrejon AB, Spain. This command was not part of the NATO air defense system, but was charged with the protection of U.S. resources in Spain. The Division also coordinated cooperation between U.S. units and the Spanish Air Force in the air defense of Spain.

The 65th AD was activated at Torrejon AB under the 16th AF on 8 April 1957, in response to a specific request from the Spanish

This F-102A (55-3451) of the 431st FIS at Prestwick, Scotland, on 15 April 1964, has the air intake splitter plate painted in White. The aircraft also has the Air Force Outstanding Unit Award ribbon painted on the fin below the unit insignia. (MAP)

government. Under the base agreements (signed in 1954), the U.S. was permitted to construct and utilize bases for deterrent forces in Spain. The construction and equipment of a Spanish Air Defense System was made a part of the base agreement.

On 1 July 1960, the 65th AD was reassigned from SAC to USAFE, because of the division's primary mission, training Spanish AF personnel in air defense tactics. The Division was unique in its integrated, side-by-side working arrangement with the Spanish AF.

USAF and Spanish AF ground controllers always worked together. The Spanish AF interceptor squadrons were commanded by the 65th AD Joint Command Post which coordinated the missions of USAF F-102As and Spanish Air Force F-86Fs.

Along with the F-102 units, the 65th also controlled a USAF Tactical Fighter Squadron on a three month rotation and seven Aircraft Control and Warning Squadrons (ACWS). The service of the F-102s ended when the air defense system was turned over to the Spanish Air Force during 1964. This came about as part of the Kennedy Administration's *Project Clearwater*. Under these budget cuts, the Spanish air defense system was turned over to the Spanish AF on 1

An F-102A (56-1163) of the 32nd FIS prepares to taxi out during the 1966 Air Defense Competition at Twente Air Base, The Netherlands. The competition was held during June of 1966. (Sectie Militaire Luchtvaart Historie RNethAF)

This F-102A (56-1062) has a Yellow and Black sunburst design on the braking parachute housing. The aircraft was assigned to the 496th FIS at Soesterberg Air Base, The Netherlands. (Author)

A TF-102A (55-4034) of the 497th FIS at Prestwick, Scotland, on 15 April 1964. The aircraft was being ferried back to the United States for issue to the 4780th ADW. (Map)

July 1964, with 65th AD being deactivated on 1 January 1965. It was reactivated in Europe during September of 1984, at Sembach AB, Germany.

Operational command of the F-102 units under NATO was exercised by the 86th Air Division (Defense), at Ramstein AB, Germany. The 86th AD had been originally formed as the Fighter Interceptor Wing on 1 July 1948 at Neubiberg AB and from 15 November 1959 until 20 May 1965, the unit was under the command of the 17th AF.

From May of 1965 until 14 November 1968, the Air Division was assigned directly to HQ USAFE. On 18 November 1960, the unit became the 86th Air Division (Defense) after the 86th FIW was combined with the ground radar functions of the 501st Tactical Control Wing. The Division controlled four F-102 squadrons and five aircraft control and warning squadrons (ACWS).

The 86th AD reported to NATO 4th ATAF, and the three FIS units based in Germany operated in Air Defense Sector 3 (the airspace over central Germany). The 32nd FIS in The Netherlands was placed under the operational command of the Royal Netherlands Air Force as part of the 2nd ATAF. Therefore, the 32nd FIS operated in Air Defense Sector 1 (the airspace over The Netherlands, north Germany and part of the North Sea).

Sometime during June of 1964, the mission of the 86th AD was changed to include not only air defense but also offensive air operations. This change was due to the assignment of the 601st Tactical Control Squadron to the Division. A year later, however, the Division reverted to the purely defensive role.

On 1 November 1968, the 496th, 525th and 526th FIS were integrated into the parent wing at their respective home bases. The USAF element at Soesterberg AB, The Netherlands, had no parent wing, and the 32nd FIS was reassigned to HQ 17th AF. On 14 Nov 1968, the 86th AD was redesignated 86th FIW and deactivated. It was activated again on 1 November 1969 as a Tactical Fighter Wing.

An F-102A-60-CO (56-1094) of the 525th FIS on the ramp at Prestwick, Scotland, on 18 May 1960. The squadron insignia was a Bulldog which earned the unit the nickname, "Bulldogs, Inc."

A tarp covers the canopy of this F-102A (56-1202) of the 526th FIS on the ramp at Ramstein Air Base, Germany, during September of 1965. The aircraft boarding ladder is in place and it appears that the canopy is slightly open. (S. Peltz)

The F-102

The Red nosed YF-102 (52-7994) was displayed on jack stands in the Convair Plant at Fort Worth, Texas, on 2 October 1953. This same facility today builds General Dynamics F-16 Fighting Falcons. (AF Logistics Command)

The Convair F-102 Delta Dagger was the airframe portion of a weapons system comprising a fire control computer, radar, communications and a battery of air-to-air guided missiles backed up by unguided rockets. Convair had been working on the concept and its related components since 1946, and expected the F-102 would be the "Ultimate Interceptor" in 1954 when it was expected to reach operational status.

The Hughes Electronic Control System (ECS), however, would not be available in time and the planned engine (the J-67) also fell far behind schedule. Finally, three years later than planned, the F-102 entered service with the USAF Air Defense Command, joining the 327th Fighter Interceptor Squadron at George AFB, California during April of 1956.

The F-102 was the first operational delta winged, all-weather interceptor capable of flying intercept missions at any hour, day or night at altitudes up to and above 50,000 feet. By September of 1958, a total of 1,000 YF-102/F-102A/TF-102A had been delivered. Of these, 168 saw service in Europe for more than eleven years. In fact, the F-102's service in Europe was for a far longer period than with the ADC in the United States.

Armament/Weapons System

Like the F-86D Sabre Dog it replaced, the F-102 carried no guns, being armed with a combination of six air-to-air missiles, Hughes GAR-1 (AIM-4) Falcons and the GAR-II (AIM-26, nuclear). Usually the combination was three AIM-4D (later AIM-4G) infrared homing and three AIM-4A (later AIM-4E) semi-active radar homing missiles.

The AIM-4D missiles were introduced in USAFE during the last quarter of 1963 after the F-102's MG-10 fire control system was modified to the FIG-8 configuration by adding an infrared sighting system. The Falcons were carried in missile bays under the fuselage with quick-opening doors. Built into the missile bay doors were launching tubes, housing 2.75 inch Folding Fin Aircraft Rockets (FFAR).

The Hughes airborne computer fire control system was tied to a ground defense system by a Data Link communications system known as SAGE in the USA and NADGE in Europe (NATO Air Defense Ground Environment). The data link allowed the ground based radar to be tied into the fighter's fire control system/auto-pilot, allowing the fighter to be automatically steered onto an interception course to the target.

The first production Convair F-102A-5-CO (53-1791) Delta Dagger lifts off the runway at Edwards Air Force Base for a test flight. During the course of its development, the F-102 would receive a completely revised fuselage. (AF Logistics Command)

Preparation for European Service

F-102s became available for deployment to Europe during 1958, 1959 and 1960 as Air Defense Command units in the United States converted to the F-101B, F-106A and newer models of the F-102A (from production blocks 80 and 90).

After the aircraft were released from the ADC squadron, they were processed through the Preparation for Overseas Transfer program (except eighteen aircraft for the 525th FIS). Ninety-three Delta Daggers went through the program at the San Antonio Air Material Area at Kelly AFB, Texas. Forty-four were serviced by the San Bernardino AMA at Norton AFB, California and nine by the Ogden AMA at Hill AFB, Utah.

One of the most troublesome aspects of the Preparation for Overseas Transfer program was the frequency with which the USAF changed the dates that various squadrons were to release or receive F-102s. As a consequence, a number of F-102s were placed in storage for periods of two to five months.

At the AMAs, the F-102s were extensively inspected and various modifications were undertaken, such as the installation of a TACAN system (Tactical Air Navigation). During FY 1960, the specifications were expanded to include the following requirements: installation of external fuel tanks, a pilot survival kit and a complete repainting (for preservation purposes). The most important modification was the upgrade of the MG-10 AWCS to the FIG-5 configuration.

Normally, an F-102 would complete the program in seventy-five days; however, Texas and California set up their FY 1960 programs on a sixty day schedule. California processed the TF-102As as well as F-102As, raising its average per aircraft to seventy-seven days. Manhours expended per aircraft ranged from 12,000 hours for a Mod/IRAN to 5,490 hours for an Overseas Transfer Inspection.

Since numerous modifications were introduced into the F-102 production program at various intervals, aircraft were produced in twenty-four different production blocks each having its own configuration. In some cases, the differences in the aircraft's wiring and components made it impossible to install later accessories. In transferring F-102s to overseas units, the program endeavored to supply each overseas squadron with just one production block configuration to simplify logistics.

After final engine and system checks, the aircraft were delivered to the port of embarkation at Brookley AFB, Alabama. The aircraft were officially assigned to the Tactical Air Command's 4440th Aircraft Delivery Group, at Langley AFB, Virginia. At Brookley AFB Mobile AMAs made the aircraft ready for surface shipment to Europe onboard aircraft carriers. This program consisted of cocooning the aircraft and was known as *Project Seaspray*.

Surface shipment normally took thirteen days. The delivery port was Saint-Nazaire, France, where the aircraft were disembarked and towed to the Sud-Aviation facility (now Aerospatiale) at Montoir Air Base. Here the F-102s were decocooned, returned to flight status, tested and ferried to their respective squadrons.

The first shipment arrived in Europe on 9 January 1959 and eventually eleven ship-loads of Delta Daggers arrived in France. The last carrier shipment arrived during October of 1960, bringing the total of surface ferried F-102s to 164 aircraft (150 F-102As and fourteen TF-102As).

On 28 January 1959, the first fighter squadron to receive the F-102 in Europe, the 525th Fighter Interceptor Squadron (FIS), took delivery of two TF-102As and three F-102As. The second unit to convert to the Delta Dagger was the 496th FIS. It received two TF-102As and two F-102As on 9 December 1959, at Hahn Air Base, Germany. The third unit was the 497th FIS, receiving its first F-102A on 26 April 1960. The fourth was 526th FIS at Ramstein Air Base. It took delivery of three F-102As on 7 June 1960. The fifth squadron was 431st FIS which took F-102A (55-3447) on strength on 28 September 1960. The sixth and last squadron was the 32nd FIS. Personnel from the 32nd FIS saw their first three F-102As land at Wheelus AB, Libya, on 12 August 1960.

These F-102As are undergoing an MG-10 AWCS operational ground check as part of the "Preparation for Overseas" program at Kelly AFB. Every component of the aircraft was checked before they were cleared for shipment. (AF Logistics Command)

F-102As (carrying 52nd FIW markings) are being overhauled as part of the "Preparation for Overseas" program at Kelly AFB, Texas. The program was run by the San Antonio AMA during May of 1960. (AF Logistics Command)

A cocooned F-102A being off-loaded from an aircraft carrier in the harbor a Saint-Nazaire, France, during January of 1959. The F-102s were transported as deck cargo and the cocoon protected the aircraft from the effects of salt air. (Aerospatiale)

Along with the F-102As, a number of TF-102As were also shipped to Europe by surface transport, arriving in France during January of 1959. The aircraft on the deck behind the TF-102 is a North American T-6 Texan trainer. (Aerospatiale)

This F-102A-70-CO (56-1255) still carries the Red tail markings of its previous squadron, the 317th FIS. The aircraft was decocooned at the Sud-Aviation facility, Saint-Nazaire, France, during January of 1959. (Aerospatiale)

When removing the cocooning from these F-102As (54-1407 and 54-1399), the aircraft's paint was damaged. Before they were issued to a squadron, the aircraft were repainted at the Sud-Aviation facility. (Aerospatiale)

Training

Although the pilots of five out of the six squadrons were qualified to fly the F-102 when assigned to their respective units, all were sent to Wheelus AB, Libya, shortly after the arrival of their aircraft. In some cases the entire squadron deployed to Wheelus, while others deployed detachments of six aircraft at a time. Normally, during a year, all squadron pilots rotated through Libya with their aircraft (although after November 1960 only in detachments of six Daggers at a time).

Since November of 1955, Wheelus Air Base, on the coast of Libya four miles east of Tripoli, had been the home of the U.S. Air Force Europe Weapons Center. The 7272nd Aircraft Gunnery Group, 17th AF, was responsible for the training and evaluation of the F-102 pilots. For F-102 gunnery training, there were two air-to-air ranges over the Mediterranean Sea between twenty and thirty miles from Tripoli. Missile and rocket firing was conducted at both high and low altitudes.

For gunnery training, radar-reflecting targets were towed by Martin B-57Es of the 7235th Support Squadron. The squadron also operated F-100Cs which were used as chase aircraft for the F-102s in training. Should a Delta Dagger's radar lock on the target tug, not the target, the order to break off was given by the chase pilot. The Delmar Radop target, built by Fairey Engineering Corp., was a highly radar reflective lightweight plastic target, reeled out over the range on a 20,000 foot cable.

During their initial F-102 training at Wheelus, pilots acquired familiarity with the GAR-1D Falcon missile and qualified on the aircraft systems. The training program was conducted by fighter interceptor officers of the TAC Operations Branch and TAC Ground Control Section.

Besides the live-firing courses at Wheelus AB, pilots also took part in continuation training. For this training, a Blue painted dummy Falcon called the Weapons System Evaluation Missile (WSEM) was used (introduced during 1960). Each squadron had a large number of WSEM missiles assigned for training purposes. In the WSEM, the rocket motor was replaced by a camera which recorded all the fire-control parameters on film at the moment the weapon was fired. The film cassette was extracted from the missile after landing and assessed as to whether a hit would have been scored. Additionally, a RADAR Recorder made a record of the fire-control radar scope presentation throughout the interception, giving the instructors a valuable training aid to debrief pilots.

This F-103A-55-CO (56-1027) of the 32nd FIS on the ramp at Wheelus Air Base, Libya, during May of 1963 is armed with two dummy Falcon missiles (WSEM) on the missile rails. These dummy rounds were used for weapons training. (J. Vadas)

Another training facility in Central Europe was introduced during October of 1967 when EB-57Es of the 4713th Defense Systems Evaluation Squadron (DSES) arrived to conduct a four week training program. A detachment worked with the F-102s of all four units of the 86th AD and with various ground radar sites. The mission of the EB-57Es was to train and test fighter crews and ground radar crews in a realistic Electronic Counter-Measure (ECM) environment. These training programs were repeated during April and October of 1968 and during February of 1969.

On 11 June 1970, Wheelus Air Base, Libya was closed when the U.S. was ordered out of Libya. To replace the Libyan training ranges, USAFE selected Zaragoza AB, Spain, and its nearby Bardenas Reales Gunnery Range as the new Weapon Training Site (beginning 19 February 1970).

Besides training at Wheelus AB, all 86th Air Division F-102 units made deployments to Torrejon AB, Spain, during the winter months. Winter weather in Germany and The Netherlands was usually bad, and the sunny skies of Spain allowed training to continue.

This TF-102A-15-CO (54-1365) of the 32nd FIS was part of the squadron training detachment that deployed to Wheelus AB, Libya, during May of 1963 for weapons training. The WSEM missile round on the forward rail is used to record the results of a firing run without actually having to fire a missile. (J. Vadas)

1st LT Raymond D. Roberts of the 525th FIS hurries from his aircraft carrying a tape recording of his mission that will be electronically analyzed to score his performance. The squadron was based at Bitburg Air Base, Germany during October of 1961. (MSGT Norman Zeisloft)

This EB-57E (55-4263) of the 4713st DSES on the taxiway at Soester-berg on 29 October 1968 was deployed to Europe to train USAFE interceptor and ground radar crews in Electronic Counter Measures (ECM) techniques. (Author)

This T-33A-10-LO (52-9833) of the 32nd FIS had the same Red-White-Blue tail markings as the unit's F-102s. The T-33 carries a radar reflecting Delmar target mounted under the wing for live fire training of F-102 crews over the North Sea. (Author)

This TF-102A-15-CO (54-1363) of the 32nd FIS was unusual in that it carried a name on the nose. The aircraft was nicknamed *BUBBLES* and also carried a pair of wooden shoes painted just below the name. (Sectie Militaire Luchtvaart Historie RNethAF)

A crewman explains the cockpit of a TF-102A-15-CO (54-1363) of the 32nd FIS to a visiting senior officer. The TF-102 was unusual for a USAF aircraft in that it featured side-by-side seating. (Sectie Militaire Luchtvaart Historic RNethAF)

F-102 Operations in Europe

An F-102A (56-1242) of the 525th FIS lands at Bitburg Air Base, Germany, on 3 October 1961. Since the German bases were so close to the enemy, the fighters were kept in a high state of readiness. (USAF)

The Fighter Interceptor Squadrons operated in Europe much the same as they had in the United States, with the unit divided into the following four sections: administration, operations, maintenance and supply.

The operations section was responsible for carrying out the unit's primary mission of air defense. It insured that the proper number of F-102s were always ready to stand alert and made sure that each pilot within the squadron maintained a high degree of proficiency.

Each FIS was linked to a number of ground radar stations through an extensive communications network. In Central Europe, NATO had divided the region in four Air Defense Sectors. Each of these sectors had its own operations center which functioned as the central coordinating agency for the units under its control. The situation in Spain during this time was similar to Central Europe, although not under NATO control.

During normal flying hours, there was always at least one flight of F-102s in the air. A normal sortie lasted approximately 1.4 hours. Along with the airborne aircraft, each squadron had two to four Delta Daggers in an alert hangar, with one pair on five minute and the other pair on fifteen minute alert (during November of 1963 this was changed to thirty minute alert). An additional two aircraft were maintained on a one hour standby.

On 3 November 1964, the alert posture was changed. Two aircraft remained on five minute alert with eight other aircraft in a standby status (within six hours) and another four as backups (within twelve hours).

The alert hangar was a permanent building, housing the fully armed F-102s in a ready to scramble condition. The standard interception unit of two aircraft could get airborne within three to five minutes of receiving the initial alarm. The Delta Daggers could be at 40,000 feet within four to four and a half minutes after takeoff.

Raymond Roberts, a former pilot with the 525th, FIS recalled an alert tour:

A normal twenty-four hour tour would usually have several scrambles where you would end up in the cockpit, ready for start when the word came to stand down. Normally, during a tour you would get at least one full scramble. The weather was never a question: we went regardless of the weather and had great pride in being true all-weather pilots.

The main peace-time task for the F-102s was the identification of unknown aircraft crossing the ADIZ (Air Defense Identification Zone), a thirty mile wide zone between the East and West. Between two and four live scrambles usually occurred each week to visually identify intruders. In most cases the unidentified aircraft turned out to be airliners off their track or off their flight plan crossing times.

A type of mission was recalled by F-102 pilot Raymond Roberts of the 525th FIS. The mission, involving several groups of three F-102s from several airfields in Central Europe, took place during 1961. The F-102s departed in two waves, some eigth minutes apart, flying toward the "Iron Curtain" at high altitude and high speed. The Delta Daggers flew as high as possible(49,000 to 50,000 feet) and fast as possible. Within a mile of the border they broke off and, nearly out of fuel, headed for the closest air field.

The purpose of the mission was to cause the WARSAW Pact air defense system to turn on their radars so that USAF Electronic Intelligence (ELINT) aircraft could locate and evaluate the units. The mission was a complete success.

Another task assigned to the F-102 units was assistance to pilots in distress, day or night. On one such mission, during late February of 1960, two F-102As of the 525th FIS scrambled to investigate two unidentified aircraft near the East German border. They turned out to be two West German F-84s lost and low on fuel. The F-102As escorted the two F-84s to a safe landing at Giebelstadt AB, Germany.

A pilot races out to his F-102A (56-1264) of the 525th FIS on the ramp at Bitburg AB, Germany. The aircraft carries commander stripes around the fuselage behind the cockpit, and crew name silhouettes on the nose. (USAF)

An F-102A Delta Dagger of the 32nd FIS takes off from Soesterberg Air Base. The aircraft has the twin antennas under the rear fuselage that identify it as a data link equipped aircraft.

In another mission, aircraft of the 525th FIS scrambled to investigate an aircraft in trouble about eighty miles from Bitburg AB. The aircraft was identified as a T-33A enroute from England to Ramstein AB, Germany , with its radio and navigational equipment out.

During 1963, the air defense radar warning and control system in Central Europe was modernized. The radar sites converted from manual plotting and tracking equipment to the 412-L AWCS (Air Weapons and Control System) equipped with data link. Under this system, all missions were directed by data link rather than by voice transmission.

The implementation, integration and the evaluation of the 412-L AWCS was coordinated by a Joint Test Center within the 86th AD. Under the code name *Gray Ghost*, some 239 sorties were flown during the second half of 1963. The 526th FIS provided forty-nine percent of the sorties, which were over and above their normal operations. For the tests, two JEF-102As were assigned to the 526th FIS during February of 1963. These aircraft were equipped with special test gear. The sortie requirements, however, quickly exceeded the capability of the two test aircraft and additional sorties had to be furnished from the 526th's normal training schedule. Final turnover to the new system took place during the Spring of 1965.

A CASA employee works on an F-102A rear fuselage being overhauled at the CASA factory in Sevilla, Spain, during October of 1963. The tail section was completely rebuilt as part of this overhaul contract. (Bob Milnes)

Modernization and Overhaul

The modernization program for the F-102 lasted several years, even after the Deuce had already began to leave USAF active service. In Europe the modernization was usually done at the home station by technical representatives or by USAF personnel from the San Antonio AMA (field teams). Additionally, there were three European factories involved on a civil contract basis.

From March of 1960 until July of 1960, twenty-four Delta Daggers of the 525th FIS along with four from the 496th FIS were repainted at the FIAT facilities in Torino, Italy. During this same period, fifty-one TF/F-102As were modernized by FIAT. The work was accomplished by teams on site at Bitburg AB (twenty-five aircraft) and Hahn AB (twenty-six aircraft). The program also included modifying the radar to the FIG-6 configuration.

From 1 July 1961 to 30 June 1962, overhaul work and modernization of F-102s was also done at the Serima Deols facility, Chateauroux AB, France. The first aircraft to arrive for the modernization program was a TF-102A (56-2333) of the 525th FIS on 1 December 1960. This was the start of the FIG-7 modification program within USAFE.

This facility was set up by the USAF/Air Material Command during 1953, and was one of five centers (four in Europe, one in Marocco). As of 15 May 1958, Chateauroux had become the central depot for the Air Material Force European Area (AMFEA). AMFEA served as the European agent for the San Antonio AMA. The overhaul contracts were issued to AMECO-Brequet as of 1 July 1958.

The work comprised the incorporation of a missile control console for the AIM-26A (nuclear) and the incorporation of electronic counter-measures (ECM) equipment. The FY62 contract was for ninety-five aircraft with each aircraft taking some forty-five days to complete. Normally, a maximum of fourteen aircraft were involved in overhaul at any one time.

Airframe and unclassified electronics modifications were done by the French contractor and classified work was carried out by USAF personnel from several units of the 86th AD. When completed, each aircraft was checked out by a WSEM check flight before it was returned to its squadron.

The Chateauroux facility also equipped all the F-102s of the 65th AD with the field arrestor hook during FY62. The aircraft of the 86th AD were modified earlier at their respective home bases.

The last Delta Dagger to go through the program at Chateauroux was an F-102A (54-1394) from the 496th FIS coming off the modification line on 12 September 1962.

On 1 July 1962, the CASA Aircraft Company at San Pablo Airport, Sevilla, Spain, was awarded a contract for modernization and IRAN work on F-102s. CASA was listed as a Specialized Repair Activity (SRA) and was involved in the F-102 program for some seven years.

The first of six prototype aircraft to go through the program was an F-102 (56-1076) of the 525th FIS, which was started on 16 April 1962. As part of the program, a complete periodic inspection was performed on all aircraft. Along with other projects, CASA also performed the F-102 1,200 hour special inspection as part of the contract.

Three different programs were undertaken at the CASA facility ranging from the latest technical modifications to repainting the aircraft. There were usually eighteen aircraft on hand at any one time and a full IRAN normally ran forty-five days. The electrical work, body repairs and general overhaul program was carried out by the Spanish employees. After the wiring was checked out and the general repairs completed, the plane was turned over to Hughes Aircraft Company personnel for installation of new radars and other electronics.

The 100th plane to complete the program at the Spanish plant was returned to the Air Force during October of 1963, following ceremonies involving MAJ Stanley L. Donovan, JUSMG Chief in Spain, and a number of Spanish officials. LTCOL J.S. Clarke Jr., commander of the 497th FIS, picked up the plane for the return flight to Torrejon Air Base.

When the last F-102 rolled out after rework on 24 Sept 1969, (F-102A 56-1264 of the 526th FIS), CASA had overhauled a total of 411 Delta Daggers. The factory president, Mr. Jose Ortig Echague, received an award from the Air Force for the outstanding quality of the company's work. The award was presented by 16th AF commander, GEN Zebailly on 11 Sept 1969.

The following modernizations were made to F-102A during the various modernization programs from 1961 through 1970:

1961: The FIG-7 program, involving the updating of the airframe, airframe electrical wiring, MG 10A aircraft and weapons control system (AWCS), and a number of other improvements and reliability modifications. This work was done at Chateauroux (beginning 1 Dec 1960). Other work done during 1961 at various locations was installation of a missile control console for the AIM-26A and installation of a field arrestor hook by field teams at each home base.

Field Arrestor Hook Program

The field arresting gear made history in Europe. It was first used in an actual emergency landing at Bitburg AB, Germany.

The prototype field arrestor hook was installed by personnel of the San Antonio AMA, during June 1960 and qualification tests were done at Edwards AFB. By the middle of July 1960, the tests had proved so successful that the Air Force issued 890 field modification kits for installation on the F-102.

In Europe, the first hooks were installed during April of 1961 at Bitburg AB.

These F-102As are being overhauled at the CASA factory in Spain. Three squadrons are represented by the six aircraft in the hangar, 56-1057/525th FIS, 56-1045/497th FIS, 56-2329/496th FIS, 54-1394/496th FIS and 56-1266/525th FIS. (Bob Milnes)

Hughes technicians overhauled the radars of the F-102As undergoing modernization and overhaul at the CASA factory. Spanish personnel were used for unclassified work, while the classified portions of the radar overhaul was performed by USAF and Hughes personnel. (Bob Milnes)

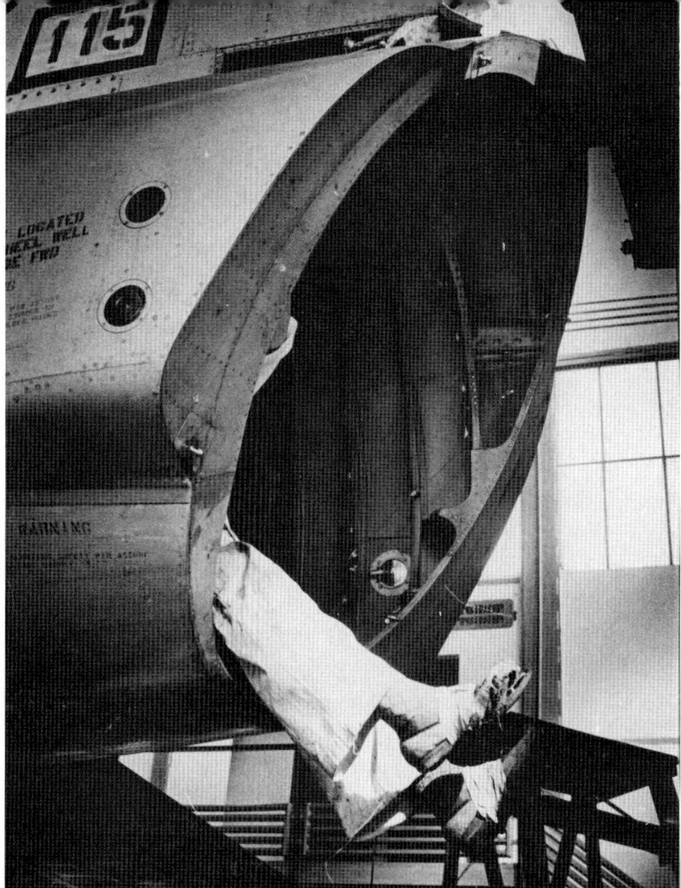

Wearing rather informal foot gear, this Spanish employee of the CASA company has really gotten into his work. The F-102A was undergoing overhaul at the CASA factory in Sevilla, Spain, during October of 1963. (Bob Milnes)

This F-102A (56-1044) of the 525th Fighter Interceptor Squadron has an infrared scanner ball mounted on the nose in front of the cockpit. This was one of the external features of aircraft that had completed the FIG-8 modification program. (Quadrant Picture Library)

The hook, hydraulically activated from the rear of the aircraft, was designed to engage a flexible steel cable running across the runway that was designed to stop the aircraft at speeds up to 160 knots. A net stretched across the runway, called the primary arresting barrier, worked in conjunction with the cable and arresting hook to halt the aircraft.

On 23 July 1963, CAPT Leslie J. Prichard of the 525th FIS successfully made the first approach-end arrestment with the hook. The second arrested landing in USAFE history was made late during March of 1964 at Ramstein AB, while Hahn AB saw their first arrestment on 19 August 1966.

1962: An automatic flight control system was added to aircraft at the CASA facility. Another modification allowed for interchangeable utilization of either the AIM-26A or AIM-4 in the center missile bay on a number of aircraft.

1963: The Hughes MG-10 fire control system was changed by the addition of an infrared Search and Track System. This was also known as the FIG-8 configuration modification, or Project Big Eight. Aircraft with this change were externally identifiable by the ball-shaped scanner housing in front of the windscreen. This work done by CASA and the 496th FIS was the first unit to receive a FIG-8 aircraft. This program was completed during September of 1964.

1964: Under project Blow Torch, the engines were modified, overhauled and the afterburners were rebuilt by CASA.

1965: The aircraft radar underwent modification to the FIG-9A configuration and a data link antenna was added at CASA (the two antenna blades were mounted under the rear of the fuselage).

1966: The infrared sub-system (FIG-10A modification) and the air weapons control system were modified.

1967: During the first half of this year all J-57-23 engines were modified by CASA at its Getafe, Spain, facility. The ejection seat underwent changes and a team from Lear-Siegler Co. modified the external tank and pylon. Anti-collision lights were added, with one Red rotating beacon being mounted on the upper fuselage spine and another under the fuselage just behind the main landing gear well. These changes were done by field teams at each home base.

1970: Shortly before the F-102 was phased out from European service, the UHF radio system was modified. The only external difference was the addition of a thin White plastic coated blade antenna on the upper forward fuselage spine, behind the cockpit. A number of F-102s from the 526th FIS were noted with this modification during April of 1970.

The small white rectangle on the air intake is the William Tell Weapons Meet emblem, which was applied to the F-102s of the 32 FIS during late 1965 after the squadron participated in the 1965 competition. (Author)

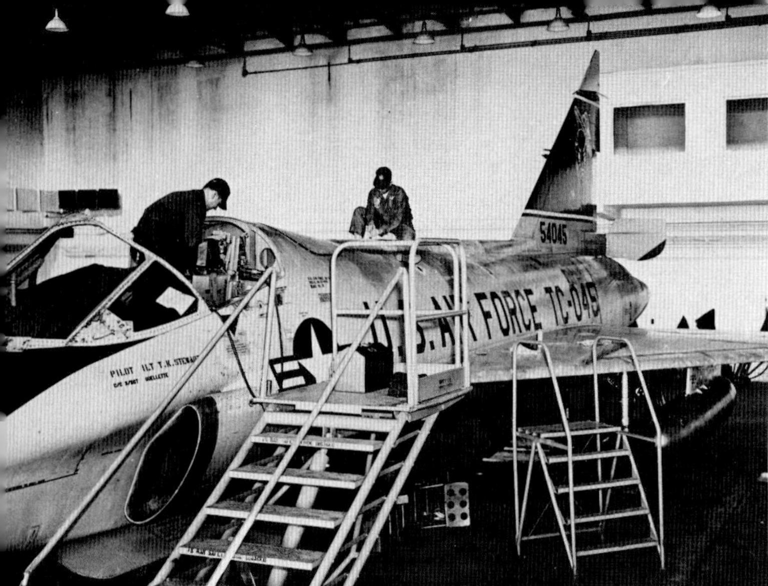

USAF maintenance technicians work on a TF-102A of the 431st FIS in the unit maintenance hangar at Zaragoza Air Base, Spain during 1964. The TF-102 was unusual for a USAF trainer in that it had side-by-side seating. (USAF Historical Research Center)

Maintenance

Good maintenance is considered to be the backbone of any fighter squadron and the ability of the maintenance section to keep the aircraft in a state of readiness determines the combat potential of the squadron.

The maintenance personnel were fully aware of the importance of their jobs. They knew that the pilots were counting on them and they knew that the F-102s in their charge would be only as good as the men who worked on them.

To keep the Delta Dagger flying, fourteen separate maintenance specialists were needed, each trained at a particular technical training school before being assigned to his squadron in Europe. Training at these schools ranged in length from eight weeks to nine months.

There were three main branches of maintenance activity for the F-102. The first was called the aircraft maintenance section, represented by the aircraft's crew chief, his assistant and the flight line chief. These men were responsible for routine day-to-day maintenance of the aircraft. The next group was the specialists, who worked on the instruments, electrical systems, hydraulics and the J-57 jet engine.

The third group included the radar/fire control technicians and the armorers, who were responsible for the missiles and rockets. Although there are three separate maintenance sections, the men worked as a team and most of the time, mechanics and technicians from different departments were working on the aircraft side by side, at the same time. An F-102 was no simple piece of equipment: it was divided into a number of distinct and separate systems and each had its separate group of maintenance men and shops to maintain them.

To assist the unit maintenance men, technical representatives (tec reps) from the factory were on hand to assist in trouble shooting maintenance problems. For the F-102 there was a ninety-two volume library of technical orders, explaining in detail each part of the aircraft. The parts catalog for the F-102 was bigger than two New York City telephone directories (1961), and contained about 2,218 pages. To assure combat ready status for each aircraft, there was a periodic maintenance check which required about 850 man hours or ten working days to accomplish. As one crewman put it, "...the aircraft maintenance man's job is never done. Rain or shine, day and night — there was always something to do."

A ground starter is hooked up to an F-102A (53-1801) of the 496th FIS on the ramp at Wheelus Air Base, Libya, during the squadron's February 1963 deployment. The starter provided high pressure air to the engine compressor and was run by its own gas engine. (Chuck Downing)

This F-102A (54-1816) of the 496th FIS on the ramp at Wheelus Air Base, Libya, has both a starter cart and an external power cart hooked up to the aircraft. Wheelus Air Base was the site for most of the weapons training conducted by USAFE squadrons. (Chuck Downing)

The F-102 silhouettes on this F-102A of the 525th FIS at Bitburg Air Base, Germany on 3 October 1961 carried the names of the pilot (upper silhouette), crew chief (lower silhouette) and assistant crew chief (bottom tail flame) in White. (MSGT Norman Zeisloft)

This emblem was painted on a number of F-102As of the 32nd FIS after the unit won the 1965 William Tell Meet. The inscription reads "USAF Fighter Weapons Meet" - "1st Place Unit"- "1965" "Fighter Interceptor." (Author)

William Tell Weapons Meet, Tyndall AFB

The William Tell WeaponsMeet, held every two years, was the USAF world-wide Fighter Interceptor Weapons Meet designed to continually evaluate tactics and weapon systems under simulated combat conditions. The meet was hosted by the Air Defense Command, USAF at Tyndall Air Force Base, Florida.

The three purposes behind William Tell were: to recognize the best aircrew-controller team in the air defense system; to demonstrate the capabilities of USAF interceptor weapons systems; and to evaluate the ability of crews to maintain, handle and load the aircraft's weapons.

There were sixteen sorties required for each team with each pilot flying four missions. Out of the sixteen sorties, twelve were live fire sorties, with missiles being fired at a Firebee drone target (both radar guided and infrared Falcons were used). Of the four sorties flown by each pilot, two were high missions (above 40,000 feet), one mission was below 1,000 feet and one mission was flown to test the pilot's ability to overcome electronic counter measures.

Participation by one of the 86th AD F-102 units was always preceded by a two-day preselection shoot-off conducted by the 86th, called "Little Willy Tell." The selection of crews for William Tell followed the same rules, competition criteria and scoring as the actual meet.

USAFE F-102 units took part in the following meets:

October of 1959, USAFE represented by the 525th FIS, came in second in the F-102 category. October of 1961, no USAFE participation because the Berlin Crisis prohibited overseas teams from participating (although the 497th FIS had been chosen to represent USAFE). October of 1963 saw the 525th FIS come in fourth in the F-102 category. The 32nd FIS won the October 1965 meet coming in first in the F-102 category against five other teams. (The meets of 1967 and 1969 were cancelled because of commitments in Southeast Asia).

AFCENT Air Defense Competition

The AFCENT Air Defense Competition was an annual competition held between NATO aircraft. The F-102 units played a significant role in these events. The first competition was held during 1965 as a continuation of the Air Firing Competitions held between 1958 to 1962 (no F-102 participation). The Air Firing meets were discontinued when interceptor armament changed from guns to missiles.

Since one of the primary roles of Air Defense units was to safeguard the integrity of their respective Air Defense region, this role was used to form the basis of the new competition. Points were awarded during subsonic and supersonic night and day events and bonus points were given for interceptions with minimum penetration of the target.

The Air Defense Competition not only scored a pilot's marksmanship, but also the skill and teamwork of pilots and intercept controllers from the various air defense sectors. Teams from different sectors competed against one another, rather than as a national team.

Central Europe was divided into four air defense sectors. Sectors 1 and 2 were under the 2nd ATAF and Sectors 3 and 4 were controlled by the 4th ATAF. The F-102s of the 32nd FIS flew for Sector 1 while those of the 496th, 525th and 526th FIS came under Sector 3. The aims of the competition were: to foster a competitive spirit between sectors, to select (under fixed rules) the outstanding controller/interceptor team and to stimulate combat proficiency training.

The competition took place over a month with each team following the schedule of events and gaining points. There was no direct confrontation between the sector teams, nor was the competition held during the same time period. The total points gained by each sector was kept secret until the last sector had completed the schedule of events.

In Sector 1, the F-102s flew as part of a multi-national team, with West German AF F-104Gs making up the other half of the team one year, RNethAF F-104Gs the next. The ground control unit was organized along the same lines, one year RNethAF, the next year a West German AF unit. Sector 3 had an all-American team during 1965 and 1966.

During 1967, AFCENT airspace was divided into three sectors, because Sector 4 had been eliminated when the French left NATO. In 1967, Sector 3 became an international team with the F-102s flying with West German AF F-104Gs, coupled with a ground control team consisting of both Germans and Americans. A Danish AF team joined the event during 1968 and in 1969, the United Kingdom Sector was included for the first time.

Three events were scheduled during the competition: a subsonic day mission (low altitude), a subsonic night mission and a supersonic day mission (high altitude). Each mission was divided into

F-102As of the 32nd FIS, together with Lockheed F-104G Starfighters of the RNethAF, prepare to taxi out during the 1966 Air Defense Competition. (Sectie Militaire Luchtvaart Historie)

MAJ Norwood Potter flies lead in F-102A 56-0983, with CAPT Goebel in F-104G JA-117 on one wing with another West German F-104 on the other wing and F-102A 56-1244 in the trail position during the 1967 Air Defense Competition. (COL Goebel, WGAF)

three phases: scramble, intercept and attack. A mission was flown by a flight of one F-102A and one F-104G (Sector 3 used only F-102As during 1965-66). There was no live-fire, the accuracy of each mission was determined through use of radar-recording tapes on the F-102s and radar scope photos on the F-104s. The radar scopes of the ground controllers were also photographed.

Each event was worth a certain number of points and there were three trophies awarded at the end of the competition: the Guynemer Trophy, presented to the winning Sector (named for CAPT Georges Guynemer, a French WW I hero, the trophy was donated by the Marcel Dassault Aircraft Company); the Hudleston Trophy, for the winning interceptor team (donated in 1965 by the Lockheed Aircraft Company); and the Burniaux Trophy, for the winning controller-team (donated by the Hughes Aircraft Company and introduced in 1966).

During the 1966 competition a fourth event was added, a medium-level day mission and during 1967 a fifth event was introduced, a turn-around and armament loading event. Also, during 1967 the Hudleston and Burniaux Trophies could be won by the Interceptor and GCI (Ground Control Intercept) teams scoring the most points even though the teams were not members of the winning sector. In 1968, a low altitude flying event was added to the competition.

Competition Rules

MAJ Wim van Breda of the Royal Netherlands Air Force, Chief-Controller of the GCI site at Den Helder, The Netherlands, was a team member of the Sector 1 team during the 1967 ADC. His account of the competition that follows was directly related to the 1967 competition, it gives a good overall view of the competition.

"The geographic area of competition was carefully determined by each sector-team, based on the location of the fighter base and the GCI site. The area formed a rectangle 400 NM by 100 NM with the airfield that was to be attacked/defended on one end. The rectangle was situated in such a way so that the GCI site could easily survey the entire area of competition. The rectangle was divided in several parts including the following: an Early-Warning (EW) line which was the farthest distance from the airfield and 400 NM from the Base line; an Initial Position (IP) line; a start line located about 120 NM from the airfield under attack; an airfield line; and finally the base line.

Each of the flying events started with two synthetic plots/

targets, because there were always two targets per event, with each of the two targets not more than ten minutes apart. Based on the speed of the plots/targets, the chief-controller had to determine which event (subsonic or supersonic) was underway. The plots/targets usually started in the area just beyond the EW line. At that moment, the Chief-controller gave the order to taxi two pairs of fighters, each consisting of one F-102A and one F-104G to the end of the runway to await the scramble order. The order was given via a telephone line, but during 1967 Sector 1 was experiencing problems with jammed phone lines and a T-33A was used as an airborne radio relay. Each second counted in the competition, especially in the event of a supersonic event.

Once the plots/targets crossed the IP line, the plot/target was directed by competition rules to hold a steady track. After proceeding twenty-three NM from the IP line, the heading of the track had to be established so that it ran parallel to the long leg of the area rectangle. The problem for the controllers was that the direction of flight of the plots/targets to the IP line was optional. Although the plot/target was visual on their radar scopes, when it would turn to make its attack run on the airfield was unknown. It was difficult for the controller to judge the best moment for scrambling the fighters. The actual intercept could only be started when the plot/target crossed the Start line. Aircraft scrambled too early had to be held within the rectangle wasting fuel (crossing lines was forbidden).

To help determine the right time to scramble, the Chief-controller had the following information available to him. During earlier training sorties, the exact time the interceptors needed to reach the Start line from the moment the scramble order was given, had been determined. This was done for each type of event (different air speeds). For an air speed of Mach 0.9, it took about eleven minutes to fly to the Start line.) This time was converted to a known distance and a formula was devised. This known time/distance could be compared to the distance of the plot/target to the IP line and when the distances were nearly equal, the interceptors were scrambled.

When the synthetic plot/target crossed the IP line, it was matched up with an actual airborne target aircraft. This aircraft has been kept in the air near the Start line and was matched into the plot/target by a target radar controller (the plot/target aircraft intercepted the synthetic plot/target on the Start line. The plot/target radar controller worked for the judges who scored the sector-team."

A TF-102A-15-CO (54-1363) of the 32nd FIS flies formation with an F-104G Starfighter (D-8053) No 306 Squadron Royal Netherlands Air Force during 1963. The Starfighter was used by a number of NATO air forces during the 1960s. (G.H. Kamphuis, RNethAF)

"The GCI controllers now had the difficult task of picking up "their plot/target" out of several plot/targets on their scope. These extra targets just happened to be near the Start line, flying in nearly the same direction and with the same speed. This extra bit of confusion was caused by other competing sector teams who sent aircraft to the area to confuse the GCI controllers. The competition area for each sector was known to the other sectors and by listening to radio conversations, they could determine the course of that particular event.

Technically, this was not allowed, but protests were always rejected because it could not be proved and the accused always denied they interfered. Again, good results depended on seconds and such tactics were rather irritating. Once the plot/target/ aircraft (and an airborne spare) had passed the Start line, the actual competition commenced. The pair of interceptors (F-102A/F-104G) were directed toward the plot/target, with both aircraft being assigned to one controller.

The F-102A had to intercept the plot/target from head-on due to its radar homing missiles, while the F-104G had to intercept from the rear to lock on with its infrared homing missiles. Both had to intercept the plot/target and the controller had to set up two different intercept techniques at the same time — a difficult task indeed. The F-102A went first and in order to gain bonus points, the intercept had to be made within a maximum of two minutes after the plot/target passed the Start line. The F-104G had a maximum of six minutes after the plot/ target passed the line to earn extra points.

The intercepts had to be run faultlessly to earn maximum points and during that time span the interceptors had to be talked into the right position, altitude, speed and distance. The interceptors could not cross the Start line (an instant disqualification) and once a plot/target crossed the Airfield line it could not be intercepted. When everything went well, the interceptor found

the plot/target and started the attack phase by radioing his GCI controller the code word "Judy," indicating that he was taking over the intercept. Hopefully, this was quickly followed by call "Splashed" indicating the plot/target was "destroyed".

With the plot/target flying supersonic and the F-102A attacking from head-on (also flying supersonic), this all took place in a matter of seconds. Considering this, the work of the controller had to be precise. During the "Night High Level" event of the 1967 competition in which the plot/target flew a speed of Mach 0.72, the F-102A splashed it in an elapsed time of twenty-six seconds.

To prove the "Splash," the radar of the F-102A was taped and the radar control scope of the F-104G was automatically photographed; at the same time, the scope at the GCI site was also photographed. The F-104G and F-102A had to keep a minimal distance of ten NM from each other throughout the whole flight (or face disqualification). This was done to avoid the chance of the F-102A and F-104G "splashing" each other. For the completion of a perfect intercept, points were gained. The controllers gained points for their set ups and the pilots gained points for the results of the attack phase. Points were lost when certain important phases of the interception were not properly completed."

MAJ Norwood Potter, pilot of F-102A (56-0983) during the 1967 ADC, recalled that there was a lot of pressure on the crews. The competition simulated combat flying as closely as possible and was very realistic. Additionally, because there were so few sorties flown, each sortie was extremely important, with no room for human error. This was reflected in the tremendous effort put forth by all team members: each member had an important job and if one failed to give 100%, the entire effort would have been futile — and no one wanted to let his team-mates down.

A pair of camouflaged F-102As of the 32nd FIS on the flight line at Twente Air Base, The Netherlands, during April of 1968. The crews are awaiting the scramble order to begin another mission during the 1968 Air Defense Competition. (G.H.J. Scharringa)

Munitions Loading Competition

USAFE was the organizer of a yearly Munitions Loading Competition known as "LOADEO." The first event was held during 1965 and representatives from each Tactical Fighter Wing, Fighter Training Wing and Fighter Interceptor Squadron within USAFE attended. The competition was divided into Classes: Class I for F-105Ds (later F-4Ds), Class II for F-100C/Ds (later F-4Cs) and Class III for F-102As. The purpose was to foster a competitive spirit between units and to select the outstanding munitions loading crew for USAFE. Trophies were given for each class, along with an overall award for the overall champion (this was eliminated in 1969). Crews were judged on loading techniques, professionalism, an inspection of equipment and a written examination. There were three loads for a maximum of 3,000 points; professionalism counted for a maximum of 300 points; equipment inspection was good for 100 points; and the written examination counted 500 points. The competition was normally held during the summer (usually July or August).

F-102 crews placed as follows during the various competitions: During 1965, the event was held at Ramstein AB and the 525th FIS took first place and the 32nd FIS came in second. The 1966 competition at RAF Lakenheath, England, saw the 525th FIS again take first place and the 32nd FIS took second. In 1967, at Ramstein AB, Germany, the 526th FIS came in first place and also took the overall trophy winner; once again the 32nd FIS came in second. During 1968, the event was held at RAF Lakenheath, with the 32nd FIS coming in first and the 525th and 526th tied for second. The 496th FIS settled for fourth place. In 1969, the competition was once more held at RAF Wethersfield, England, with the 525th FIS in first place, the 496th FIS in second place and the 526th FIS in third (the 32nd FIS had converted to the F-4E).

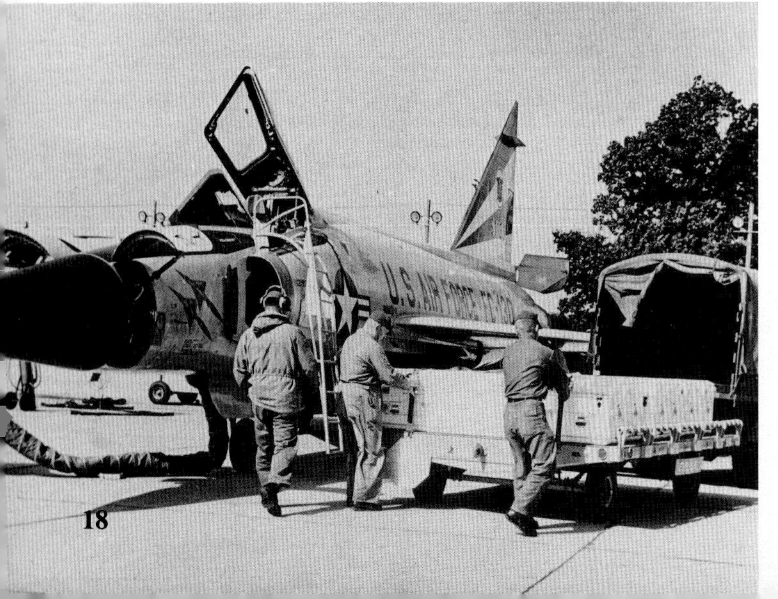

Armament technicians prepare to load missiles onto an F-102A (56-1130) of the 525th FIS at Bitburg, Germany, on 3 October 1961. The containers on the dolly each held one Falcon air-to-air missile. (USAF)

F-102 General Colors

On their arrival at Saint-Nazaire, most of the F-102s were in overall Air Defense Command Gray, although a few aircraft received by the 525th FIS carried the Arctic Red fins used by their former unit, the 317th FIS, Alaskan Air Command. Unit markings were introduced several months later with the 525th, being the first to apply their unit insignia to both sides of the vertical fin.

During 1960, all units assigned to the 86th Air Division added a sunburst marking to the vertical fin, making full use of the F-102's trianglar shaped tail. The sunburst design was applied in the squadron colors. A number of aircraft also had their respective unit markings applied to the fin, superimposed on the sunburst design.

Another marking used during this period was two Delta Dagger silhouettes carried on the port side of the nose (German based units only). These were in different colors and carried the names of the pilot and crew chief assigned to the aircraft. This marking system was initiated by MAJ Barton of the 525th FIS during 1959. The markings remained in use until the Summer of 1964. The 32nd FIS did not use silhouettes but had a number of their aircraft painted with a nose marking consisting of two wooden shoes (a Dutch tradition). These markings were in use until the Summer of 1963.

During the Summer of 1963, the F-102 units of the 86th started to remove the sunburst tail markings in connection with the FIG-8 modification program. From late 1963 until the Autumn of 1964, the F-102s flew with plain Gray fins with the unit insignia usually carried on the center of the fin. On or about the 25 March 1964, the 86th AD insignia was added to the starboard side of the tail, while the squadron insignia was carried on the port side. The various unit insignias were actually painted on the fins instead of using costly machine manufactured decals ($60 each). Stencils of sheet metal plates were made by the 7030th Field Maintenance unit at Ramstein AB and the insignias were painted on with ordinary spray enamel. The 525th and 526th FIS both used the braking parachute housing to indicate the aircraft's flight assignment (Red, Blue or White) while the 32nd FIS painted the housing Red/White/Blue after the Dutch national flag.

During late 1964, another colored fin scheme was introduced by the 86th AD. A horizontal band was added to the fin in the same squadron colors as the early 1960 period, except for the 32nd FIS, which used Green instead of Red/White/Blue (the braking parachute housing remained in these colors). This horizontal band was removed during Autumn of 1966.

In late 1965, the F-102s began to receive a camouflage paint scheme consisting of Tan, Dark Green and Medium Green upper-surfaces over Light Gray undersurfaces. The first camouflaged USAFE F-102 was aircraft 56-1214 of the 525th FIS which returned from overhaul at the CASA facility in Spain on 19 October 1965. The last Deuce to be camouflaged was a TF-102A (54-1367), which returned to the 526th FIS on 5 July 1968.

This F-102A-60-CO (56-1099) of the 431st FIS on the ramp at Zaragoza Air Base, Spain, during 1961 carries an early style of squadron insignia on the fin. (USAF via S. Chianese)

All 86th Air Division aircraft carried sunburst tail markings like this F-102A-50-CO (55-3454) of the 32nd FIS at Soesterberg Air Base during June of 1963. The use of this fin marking was halted during the late Summer of 1963. (Author)

This F-102A-55-CO (56-1006) of the 32nd FIS has a plain Gray fin with a Red, White and Blue braking parachute housing. This style of markings was common from late 1963 through the Autumn of 1964. (Author)

An F-102A (56-1107) of the 525th Fighter Interceptor Squadron taxies along the taxiway at Soesterberg Air Base, The Netherlands, during a visit on 29 October 1965. (Author)

This TF-102A Delta Dagger of the 526th FIS on the taxiway at Soesterberg Air Base, The Netherlands, on 19 July 1966 is unusual in that it has a thin White band between the radome and anti-glare panel on the nose. (Author)

The F-102 silhouettes on the nose of this weathered F-102A (54-1399) of the 496th FIS at Soesterberg Air Base, The Netherlands, during September of 1963 carried the names of the pilot and crew chief in White. (Author)

This F-102A (56-1046) of the 496th FIS has a Yellow fin band with the 86th Air Division insignia on it. The braking parachute housing is in Yellow and Black. The aircraft was visiting Soesterberg Air Base on 24 June 1966 (Author)

A pair of camouflaged F-102A-55-COs (56-1023 and 56-1002) of the 32nd FIS on final approach for landing at Soesterberg on 27 May 1969. The first camouflaged F-102s arrived in USAFE during October of 1965. (H.De Ree)

The 32nd Fighter Interceptor Squadron

The 32nd FIS had the unique position of being the only flying unit in the USAF under the direct operational control of a foreign nation, namely the Royal Netherlands Air Force. This was done to underline the mutual goodwill and trust between the United States and her NATO partners. Actually, as is the case throughout NATO, the command structure was a multi-national affair.

Operationally, the 32nd was directly responsible to the Sector Commander of the RNethAF, who in turn reported to the 2nd ATAF commander. A NATO study concerning allied air defenses, resulted in a recommendation to improve and bolster the Central European Area with an extra fighter squadron. As a result the 32nd FIS was assigned to the RNethAF as part of the NATO air defense system.

The 32nd FIS had links to the Dutch and had been stationed on the Dutch West Indies island of Curacao during the Second World War. The unit was reactivated at Soesterberg Air Base, the Netherlands, on 8 September 1955. The American controlled part of Soesterberg AB was unofficially renamed, "Camp New Amsterdam," another reference to Dutch-American history (New Amsterdam was the original Dutch settlement in the United States, now known as New York City).

To indicate the squadron's association with the Dutch, the squadron patch was superimposed inside a wreath and crown device during 1959. The crown symbolized royalty, and the wreath with oranges represented an orange tree — the traditional symbol of the Dutch Royal Family (the House of Orange). An official application to adopt the crest as the unit's official insignia was sent to President Dwight D. Eisenhower who approved the insignia. The squadron was later referred to as the first "Royal United States Squadron" in the world. The emblem itself was designed by the Walt Disney Studios and represented a Wolfhound. A motto — Honor, Courage, and Vigilance — was adopted some fourteen years later on 16 May 1969.

The F-102 Years

The 32nd FIS was the only squadron within USAFE which had no pilots qualified in the F-102 when the aircraft arrived in Europe. As a result, the Daggers were sent to Wheelus AB, Libya (with the first three aircraft arriving on 12 August 1960). There the F-102s were

A ground crewman checks the cockpit of a F-102A-55-CO (56-1042) of the 32nd FIS on the ramp at Soesterberg Air Base on 6 January 1961. (Sectie Militaire Luchtvaart Historie RNethAF)

assigned to the 86th FIW. The transition of the squadron's twenty-two pilots began on 5 Sept 1960. Four were former F-86D Sabre Dog pilots and eighteen were former F-100C Super Sabre pilots. A total of twenty-four pilots were assigned to the 32nd FIS and were brought up to alert ready status during the unit's deployment to Wheelus AB. During the transition training period, a total of 1,200 flight hours and 1,050 sorties were flown.

The transition was completed on 17 November 1960 and all aircraft were officially handed back to the 32nd FIS at Wheelus AB on 18 November 1960. The first group of eight F-102As arrived back at Soesterberg AB on 17 December 1960 after a two day flight from Wheelus AB. A second group of nine Delta Daggers landed at Soesterberg on 19 December and the remaining three arrived during January of 1961.

On 9 February 1961, the 32nd FIS was declared operational and put two aircraft on five minute alert. During this ceremony, two F-102As were scrambled for the first time from the new alert hangars (each housing two Delta Daggers). The 32nd FIS operated with RNethAF Hawker Hunter F.Mk.6 aircraft of the No 325 Squadron which was also based at Soesterberg.

During July of 1963, the commander of the 32nd FIS, LTCOL G.S. Nicely, proposed the joint use of the alert hangar by both 32nd and No 325 aircraft. This arrangement became effective on 1 November 1963 and ended during 1966.

During October of 1962, a number of squadron aircraft deployed to Wheelus for weapons training, but the deployment was cut short (after a week and a half) due to the Cuban Missile Crisis. Once the crisis had passed, they returned to Wheelus AB on 27 April 1963. Four flights of six aircraft each spent a week undergoing weapons training and during this period the 32nd claimed a new record for successful intercepts. The previous record was set by the 497th FIS during May of 1962 (a success rate of 85.12 percent). The new record, set by Red flight (led by CAPT Kenneth C. Schow) was 90.16 percent. During the qualifications, BGEN Frank W. Gillespie, commander of the 86th Air Division, flew with Red flight and fired a missile.

A line up of F-102As (56-1032, 56-1028, 56-1043, 56-1042, 56-0993, 56-0996, 56-0982 and 56-1029) of the 32nd FIS on the ramp at Soesterberg Air Base, The Netherlands, during late 1960 or early 1961. The fin markings were Red/White/Blue. (Sectie Militaire Luchtvaart Historie RNethAF)

This F-102A-55-C (56-1043) of the 32nd FIS has some of the Air Defense Command Gray paint peeling off the fuselage. The harsh winters in The Netherlands were hard on the aircraft.

A flight of F-102As (56-1028 and 56-1032) of the 32nd FIS join up on a flight of two Hunters F.6s and a Hunter T.7 trainer No 325 Squadron, RNethAF, over The Netherlands during September of 1962. (Sectie Militaire Luchtvaart Historie RNethAF)

One of the more outstanding aspects of the squadron's performance at Wheelus AB was the low percentage of intercepts lost due to pilot error. The squadron's maintenance personnel were singled out as the backbone of the operation. The radar section also had one of the lowest rates of lost intercepts due to radar failures that had ever been recorded at Wheelus.

In one instance, five out of six specific aircraft had to be ready in a short period of time and four of them were in need of systems repairs. In readying these aircraft, one crew removed and replaced a radar transmitter and receiver unit and realigned the receiver in the aircraft in just twenty minutes, a job which normally requires two hours.

During early 1964, all 32nd FIS aircraft were modified with the infrared detection and tracking system. This major improvement in target tracking and detection, gave the MG-10 system a much greater effectiveness at low altitudes and in an ECM environment. The use of this infrared sub-system was included in the unit's training requirements. The 32nd FIS also worked out an agreement with the RNethAF and the 10th TRW to provide ECCM training targets, usually RB-66Cs, with an average of two ECCM (Electronic Counter-Counter Measures) target flights being flown per week (beginning in March of 1964).

During January of 1966, the 32nd deployed to Torrejon AB, Spain, for the first time to take advantage of the better weather conditions for training. There training period covered 151 sorties flown by six aircraft (241 flying hours). This training cycle was repeated during March of 1967 when six F-102As flew an average of ten sorties per day, for a total of 190 flight hours. While the winter weather conditions at Soesterberg AB were bad, the deployments to Spain were also conducted because practice deployments were required USAF training procedures.

Another deployment was made (with six aircraft) during Autumn of 1966 to Erding Air Base, Germany. In January of 1967, the squadron deployed six F-102s to stand alert at Erding because a Soviet MiG-17 had landed in Bavaria. While at Erding, fifteen missions were flown. Erding AB again hosted six 32nd aircraft during May of

1967. This deployment was in connection with proficiency training with the 412-L semi-automatic radar system.

The 32nd participated in the 1965 William Tell Meet and was the first USAFE unit to fly its own aircraft back to the continental U.S. The over water deployment started on 15 September 1965 and ended when the six F-102As arrived back home on 15 October.

The six aircraft first flew to Perrin AFB, Texas, for a two week training and check-out period. Aircraft 56-1023, -1032, 1130, and -1163 actually flew the Meet, while 56-1211 and -1244 were parked at Eglin AFB. Under the rules of the meet, the aircraft could not be changed once the competition commenced.

At the end of the eight-day event, the 32nd FIS won in the F-102 category with a total score of 8,782 points and took first place after a "photo-finish" against the 59th FIS. The Richard I. Bong Trophy was presented to the team leader, CAPT Erwin P. Wallaker, marking the first time an overseas entry had won. Also, it was noted that this was the first time a squadron had been directed to victory by foreign controllers (RNethAF CAPT Paul Bakker was the controller team leader). The maintenance chief and leader of the contingent was CAPT Richard W. Scott.

Several congratulatory speeches were heard at Soesterberg AB when the flight returned on 15 October, after a total of 230 flying hours (including the ferry time). Later, several aircraft flew with a special marking under the cockpit that read: "1st Place Unit, 1965 Fighter Interceptor."

On 15 February 1968, the 32nd set a USAFE and possibly a USAF record for an F-102 turn around of seven minutes thirty-two seconds. The record turnaround was a closely coordinated action overseen by a turnaround director, and performed by a four-man load crew, a crew chief and two assistant crew chiefs.

The F-102 manual specifies that a turnaround should be completed in fifteen minutes or less. This particular turnaround started when an F-102 was scrambled with a weapons system evaluation missile (WSEM). The turnaround crew was alerted some thirty minutes before the aircraft was due to return. When the F-102 landed, it went through a cursory inspection area where a crew chief

A pair of F-102As (56-1028 and 56-1032) of the 32nd FIS fly formation with a pair of Hawker Hunter F. 6s of No 325 Squadron, Royal Netherlands Air Force (RNethAF) during September of 1962. The two units shared the RNethAF base at Soesterberg. (Sectie Militaire Luchtvaart Historie RNetnAF)

This F-102A (56-0975) of the 32nd Fighter Interceptor Squadron on the taxiway at Soesterberg Air Base, The Netherlands, on 13 July 1964 carries a large squadron insignia on the fin. (Author)

This TF-102A-150-CO (54-1363) of the 32nd FIS at Soesterberg on 21 July 1965 carries the 86th Air Division badge on starboard side of the fin. The braking parachute housing is Red, White and Blue. (Author)

checked the aircraft for mechanical problems and armament personnel removed the WSEM and inspected the aircraft's launcher rails. The aircraft then taxied to the turnaround area. Turnaround time starts as soon as the wheel chocks were in place.

During the turnaround, six missiles and twelve 2.75 inch rockets were loaded on the aircraft. At the same time, the F-102 is refueled and the nitrogen and oxygen systems are replenished. A new dragchute was installed, the entire hydraulic system was checked and the oil reservoirs refilled if needed. Then, when the pilot returns, a visual inspection of the entire aircraft plane was made, checking for leaks, worn tires, or any other malfunctions. The pilot then climbs into the cockpit and leaves immediately.

Impressive as it was, the turnaround record was later bettered. The new record was seven minutes, twenty seconds and was set during May of 1969.

Competitions

Participation in competitions are always a good way to better unit morale and improve the already high quality of flight operations. With an exception of the William Tell meet, all other competitions in which the F-102s took part were held during the second half of the 1960s.

During 1966 and 1967, the 32nd FIS came in first in the NATO/AFCENT Air Defense Competition. During 1965, Sector 1 (with the 32nd FIS) lost first place because of a radar failure during a night mission, and had to settle for second place.

The 1968 LOADEO Competition was also very successful for 32nd FIS crews. The team recorded the fastest times and the highest scores of all the participants in the F-102 category. It won the Trophy by a wide margin with a total of 3,403 points. To get ready for the event, the loading crew had practiced for about five weeks.

Awards

On 21 October 1965, the Department of the Air Force announced that the 86th Air Division had won the Air Force Outstanding Unit Award for the period 1 July 1964 to 30 June 1965. The 32nd, as part of the 86th AD shared in the award. It was the 32nd's second AFOUA (1958). The squadron was the only air defense unit within AFCENT

An F-102A-55-CO (56-0985) of the 32nd FIS taxies back to the ramp at Soesterberg after a mission during November of 1964. The 32nd was the only USAF fighter squadron to serve under the operational control of a foreign air force. (Author)

to receive the outstanding unit evaluation rating of 1, when the 2nd ATAF conducted an operational evaluation during April of 1966.

The 1966 "Hughes Achievement Award" was presented to the 32nd on 8 Dec 1966 as the most outstanding air defense unit in the USAF. The 32nd beat other fighter interceptor units from the Alaskan Air Command, USAFE, Pacific Air Forces and the Air National Guard. The Award was sponsored by the Hughes Aircraft Company and had been presented annually since 1953 by Headquarters U.S. Air Force.

Colors

The Red-White-Blue fin markings were added to the aircraft while the aircraft were at Wheelus AB. During 1961, a few of the unit's F-102s began to carry small squadron emblems on both sides of the fin.

In 1962 more than half of the assigned aircraft had these markings. One TF-102A (54-1363) was noted with name **Bubbles** on the nose

This F-102A of the 32nd FIS on the track at Soesterberg on 11 August 1965 has a Red, White and Blue flash painted on the underwing drop tanks along with the same colors on the braking parachute housing. (Author)

This TF-102A-15-CO (54-1365) of the 32nd FIS was being returned to the United States and had staged through Prestwick, Scotland, on 15 April 1964. The only markings are the Red, White and Blue flashes on the braking parachute housing. (MAP)

This F-102A-55-CO (56-0987) of the 32nd FIS has a Red, White and Blue flash on the drop tank. The aircraft also has the 86th Air Division insignia painted on the starboard side of the fin. (Author)

(early 1962 until the Summer of 1963). The squadron also used a wooden shoe marking on the nose which was introduced during 1962. At least half of the squadron's aircraft carried this marking until the Summer of 1963.

During the Summer of 1963, the Red-White-Blue fin markings were moved to the drag parachute container doors. None of the aircraft carried the squadron insignia, with the exception of aircraft 55-3456 which carried a small unit insignia on the tail until the aircraft returned to the U.S. during June of 1964.

In June of 1964, six squadron aircraft were painted with the unit insignia on one side of the fin and the insignia of the 86th AD on the other side. Four F-102As (with another two as stand-bys) were repainted in time to participate in the change of command ceremonies at Ramstein AB, Germany on 10 July 1964. These aircraft were 56-0975, -0980, -0985, -0993, -1006 and -1013. On 1 Oct 1964, aircraft 56-1032 also was repainted with the insignias.

This aircraft was also painted with a Red-White-Blue commander's band across the fuselage. The squadron lost this aircraft to the 525th FIS on 10 January 1964, but because of its unique serial number, the squadron requested its return and the aircraft was reassigned on 4 Sept 1964.

The unit insignia were again removed from the fin during November of 1964 (except for 56-1032 and -1013). On 25 February 1965, the commander's band on 56-1032 was changed, becoming more angled and ending at the wing root. The squadron emblems were added once more on the tail of this aircraft during June of 1965. The eighth aircraft to fly with a squadron emblem on the fin was 56-1236 (June to December of 1965).

On 10 August 1965, a distinctive Green band, bordered in White was added to the vertical fin. The band also carried a small 32nd FIS insignia on the port side and the 86th AD insignia on the starboard side. The brake parachute housing was still colored Red-White-Blue. This scheme was first introduced on aircraft 56-0977. A total of twenty aircraft were repainted with the Green band.

On 30 October 1965, F-102 56-1122 returned from overhaul by CASA in Spain in a camouflaged scheme. By the end of 1966, nine

This F-102A (56-1245) of the 32nd FIS was formerly flown by the 526th FIS. The lighter spot on the fin is where the 526th unit insignia was overpainted with a lighter shade of Gray paint which did not match the rest of the fin. (Author)

other 32nd F-102s were camouflaged. The last Dagger to be repainted in camouflage was 56-1013 and it returned to Soesterberg AB on 2 February 1968.

Aircraft Accidents

The 32nd had the lowest attrition rate of the four F-102 units within the 86th AD. The 32nd lost only two aircraft in flying accidents. 56-1021 crashed on 25 September 1961 and 56-0973 crashed on 12 December 1962. 1st LT. C. Robert Henderson ejected after a missed approach.

A third aircraft loss occurred on 2 August 1966, when 56-1029 burned due to a fire in one of the alert hangars. The aircraft caught fire during engine start and the aft-section was quickly engulfed in flames. The pilot, rescued by the crew chief, and the other aircraft of the scramble pair was saved. The other pair of Deuces in the other half of the alert hangar was also saved along with their servicing equipment (despite the hazards of exploding fuel and ammunition aboard the burning aircraft). As a result of their actions during this incident, two officers and three enlisted men were presented the Airmen's Medal on 10 March 1967.

There were two other incidents involving F-102s. On 12 September 1960, TF-102A (54-1365) was damaged in a hard landing at Wheelus when the instructor-pilot misjudged the aircraft's altitude over the runway. Another mishap occurred on 13 April 1961 during a night interception of a Royal Netherlands Air Force Hunter. The aircraft collided, with the Hunter crashing while the damaged F-102 was able to make a safe landing.

The reliability of the F-102 allowed the 32nd to achieve an impressive flying safety record, especially over its last three years. Between August of 1966 and July of 1969, the 32nd flew 13,500 hours without an accident.

Phase Out

The 32nd never saw combat and no kills were recorded, except for two deer that tried to cross the runway during a night landing. As a record of the "kills," the aircraft, flown by 1st LT Thomas C. See, was marked with silhouettes of two deer and named "Deer Slayer."

During June of 1969, nine pilots of the 32nd completed conversion training in the F-4E Phantom at Homestead AFB. The rest of the pilots for the F-4E were newly assigned and while the pilots were training, the Daggers were flown by pilots from the Air National Guard under Operation PALACE ALERT.

On 1 July 1969 the 32nd was redesignated as a Tactical Fighter Squadron and on 2 July, twelve aircraft left Soesterberg AB. On 3 July, the last nine F-102s, were ferried to the U.S. and handed over to the 132nd FIS at Bangor, Maine, under project *Coronet East 80*.

Many members of the 32nd FIS had mixed emotions when the last of the squadron's Delta Daggers left Soesterberg. The pilots appreciated the F-102's smoothness and stable flight and its excellent safety record. The maintenance crews remembered the satisfying feeling of hearing afterburners light with a "bang" and watching "their birds" lift off the runway.

The first two F-4E Phantom IIs assigned to the 32nd Tactical Fighter Squadron landed at Soesterberg on 5 August 1969, ending an era.

A TF-102A-25-CO (54-1370) of the 32nd FIS taxies along the taxiway of Soesterberg Air Base, The Netherlands, on 18 August 1965. The braking chute housing has bands of Red, White and Blue. (W. Snel)

Later the 32nd FIS added a Green band to the fin. This TF-102A-25-CO (54-1370) carried the 86th Air Division badge on the starboard side and the unit badge on the port side. (W. Snel)

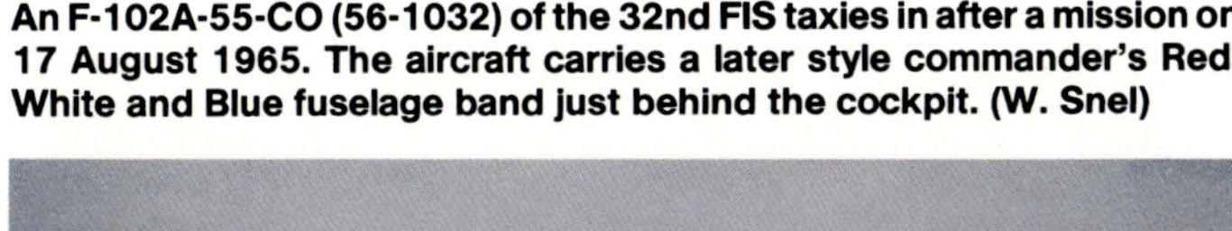

An F-102A-55-CO (56-1032) of the 32nd FIS taxies in after a mission on 17 August 1965. The aircraft carries a later style commander's Red, White and Blue fuselage band just behind the cockpit. (W. Snel)

This F-102A-55-CO (56-0993) of the 32nd FIS at Soesterberg during October of 1964 has the unit patch painted on the fin above the aircraft serial number. (W. Snel)

This F-102A-55-CO (56-1032) was flown by the commander of the 32nd FIS on 5 November 1964 and is painted with the Red, White and Blue commander's stripes behind the cockpit. The emblem on the fin is the badge of the 86th Air Division. (W. Snel)

This F-102A-55-CO (56-0996) of 32nd FIS has a wooden shoe marking on the nose. The unit was stationed at Soesterberg Air Base in The Netherlands, during July of 1962.

Four F-102A Delta Daggers of the 32nd Fighter Interceptor Squadron parked on the ramp at Prestwick Airport, Scotland on 1 June 1964. The anti-glare panel and radome are Flat Black.

During mid-1965, USAFE F-102 units were directed to paint the fins of their F-102s with a colored horizontal band. Additionally, this aircraft is not carrying large Black buzz numbers on the fuselage sides. (Author)

The large Black numbers on the fuselage sides of this F-102A of the 32nd FIS were known as Buzz Numbers and were designed to discourage low flying by USAF personnel. Civilians were encouraged to report the number of any low flying USAF aircraft. (Author)

The unit insignia of the 32nd Fighter Interceptor Squadron was designed by the Walt Disney studios and represented a Wolfhound. This F-102A at Soesterberg on 12 August 1965 also had the 86th Air Division insignia on the other side of the fin. (Author)

The fin band on this F-102A Delta Dagger of the 32nd FIS is Green with a White outline. The aircraft carries the squadron insignia on the band. The stripe around the rear fuselage was Red and marked the position of the engine turbine blades. (Author)

The infrared scanner ball on the nose of this F-102A-70-CO (56-1236) marks it as one of the aircraft that completed overhaul and modernization. The aircraft belongs to the 32nd FIS. (Author)

A Delta Dagger of the "Wolfhounds," the 32nd Fighter Interceptor Squadron. The unit was also known as the only "Royal" fighter squadron in the USAF because of the crown device carried on its unit insignia. (Author)

This F-102A of the 32nd FIS is unusual in that it carries two natural metal underwing drop tanks. Most of the drop tanks used with the F-102s were painted in the same color as the aircraft, overall ADC Gray. (Author)

An F-102A-55-CO of the 32nd FIS climbs out from Soesterberg Air Base, on 18 July 1966. The aircraft carries the 86th Air Division badge on the Green fin band, with a Red, White and Blue braking parachute housing. (Author)

This pitot tube on this F-102A of the 32nd FIS is painted with Red and White stripes to make it more visible on the ground. The aircraft also has a Red, White and Blue flash painted on the underwing drop tanks. (Author)

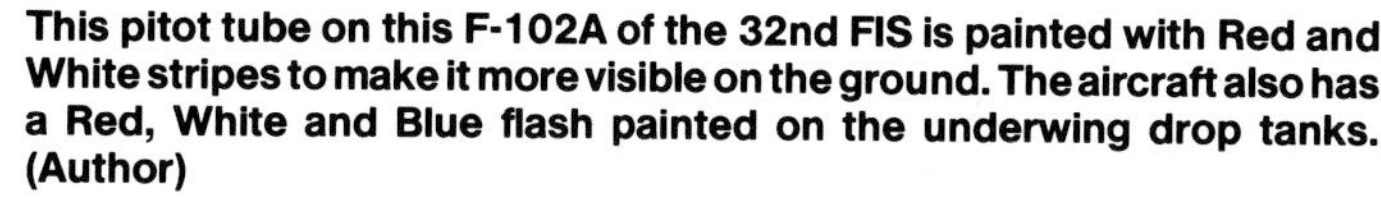

The braking parachute housing on this F-102A of the 32nd FIS is Red, White and Blue. This area was not always painted and the squadron operated a number of Delta Daggers both with and without the painted housing. (Author)

A Delta Dagger pilot taxies his F-102A-55-CO of the 32nd FIS along the taxiway of Soesterberg Air Base, The Netherlands on 7 April 1966. The 32nd shared the base with a Royal Netherlands Air Force Hawker Hunter fighter squadron. (Author)

A lineup of F-102s of the 431st Fighter Interceptor Squadron on the ramp at Wheelus Air Base, Libya, during July of 1962. The third aircraft in line is the squadron commander's aircraft. (S. Chianese)

This F-102A-55-CO (56-1006) of the 431st FIS on the ramp at Zaragoza Air Base, Spain, during April of 1962 carries special markings on the braking parachute housing identifying it as the squadron commander's aircraft. (S. Chianese)

In addition to the colored braking parachute housing, this F-102A-55-CO (56-1006) flown by the commander of the 431st FIS also had a commander's band on the fuselage that consisted of three Red bands against a White background. (S. Chianese)

The commander's band on this F-102A-40-CO (54-1405) of the 496th FIS at Hahn AB, Germany, during the early 1960s is unusual in that it is carried on the nose. (D. Menard)

The colors of the 496th FIS were Black and Yellow. This F-102A-60-CO (56-1062) at Soesterberg Air Base, on 13 August 1965 has those colors painted on the intake plate, braking parachute housing and fin band. (A.G. v.d. Brink)

An F-102A-60-CO (56-1095) of the 496th FIS taxies in at Soesterberg Air Base, The Netherlands, on 13 August 1965. The aircraft is unusual in that it is not carrying the squadron badge on the fin band. (A.G. v.d. Brink)

The squadron commander's F-102A-60-CO (56-1080) of the 496th FIS carried a Red, Yellow and Blue commander's band on the fuselage and a spiral band on the wing tanks during August of 1964. (G. Pennick)

The band around the air intake on this F-102A-65-CO of the 32nd FIS is polished natural metal. The dark areas on the top of the air intakes were painted Flat Black like the anti-glare panel on the nose. (Author)

This F-102A has a commander's band around the fuselage behind the cockpit and a William Tell Weapons Meet emblem on the air intake. The aircraft also appears to have a Black bird personal insignia on the nose. (Author)

The small White panel on the nose of this F-102A of the 32nd FIS was the armament panel. Loading crews would write what types of missiles the aircraft was armed with on this panel in Black grease pencil. (Author)

An F-102A Delta Dagger of the 32nd FIS climbs out after overshooting its landing at Soesterberg Air Base, on 10 December 1966. This aircraft has both the twin data link antenna modification under the rear fuselage and the infrared scanner dome on the nose ahead of the cockpit. (Author)

A pair of Delta Daggers of the 32nd FIS scramble from Soesterberg Air Base on 10 August 1967. The aircraft will be directed to their target via data link information relayed from the GCI site. (Author)

This F-102A-55-CO (56-1014) of the 32nd FIS has the braking parachute fully deployed while landing at Soesterberg Air Base on 7 April 1967. Once the aircraft slowed, the parachute was dropped and was picked up by ground crews. (Author)

A camouflaged F-102A-55-CO of the 32nd FIS climbs out from Soesterberg Air Base on 12 June 1967. While the camouflage was effective for low level operations, it made the interceptors stand out at high altitudes. (Author)

This F-102A-65-CO of the 32nd FIS has been modernized with a field barrier arresting hook and twin data link antennas under the rear fuselage. (Author)

32nd F.I.S.

AUG. 1960 - JUNE 1963

JUNE 1963 - AUG. 1965

AUG. 1965 - DEC. 1966

496th F.I.S.

MAY 1960 - AUG. 1963

AUG. 1963 - JUNE 1964

JULY 1964 - NOV. 1966

431st F.I.S.

DEC. 1961 - JUNE 1964

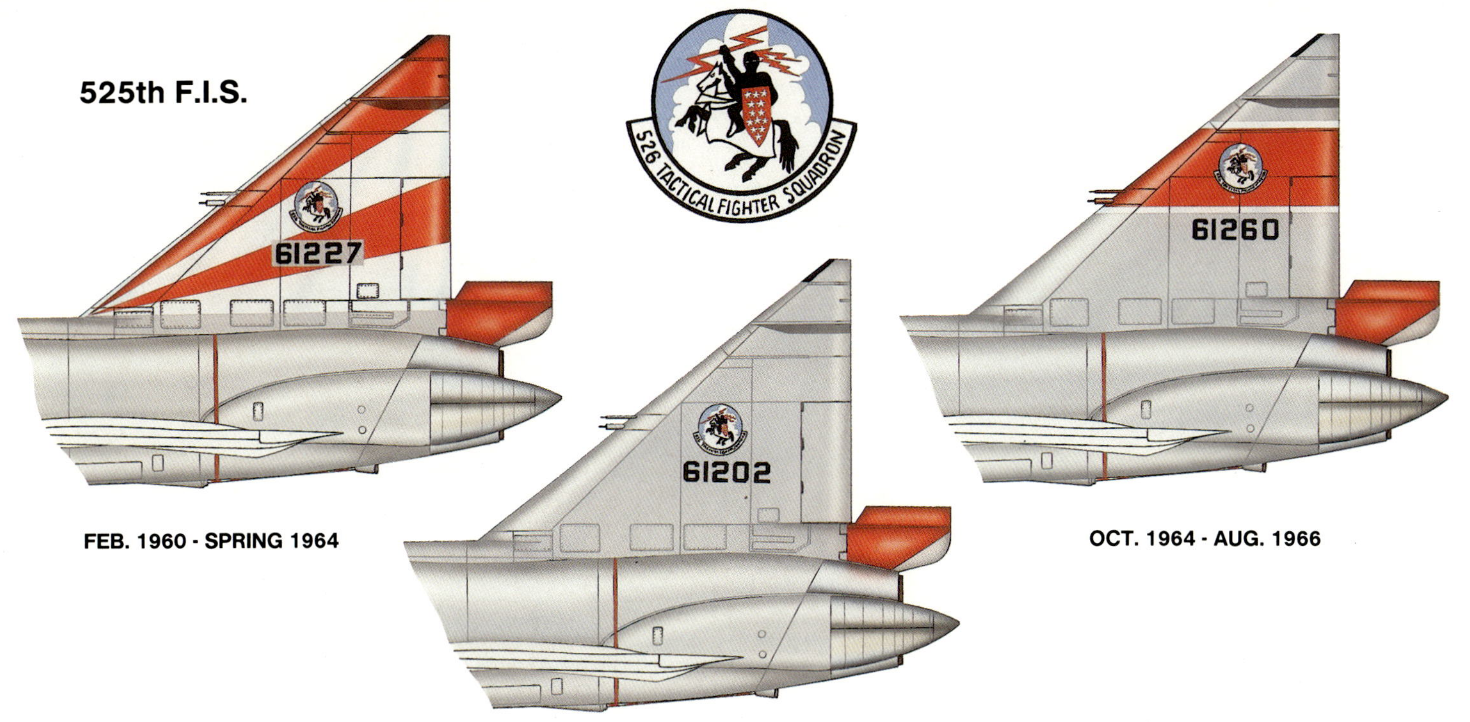

525th F.I.S.

526 TACTICAL FIGHTER SQUADRON

61227

FEB. 1960 - SPRING 1964

61202

SPRING 1964 - OCT. 1964

61260

OCT. 1964 - AUG. 1966

526th F.I.S.

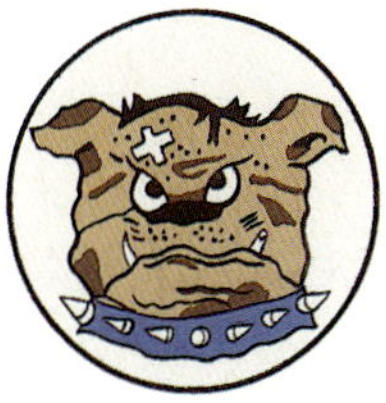

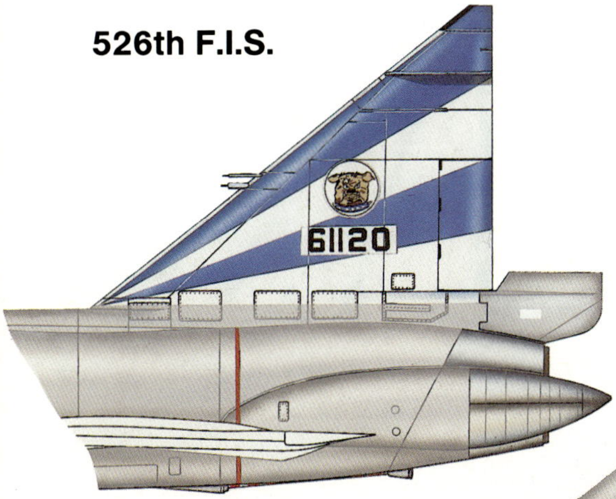
61120

1961 - OCT. 1963

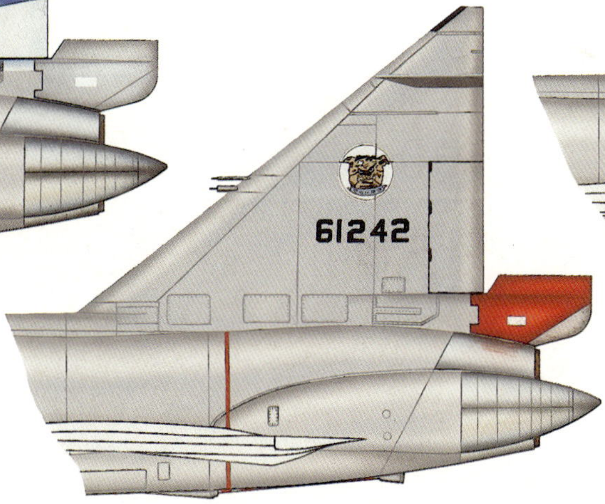
61242

OCT. 1963 - NOV. 1964

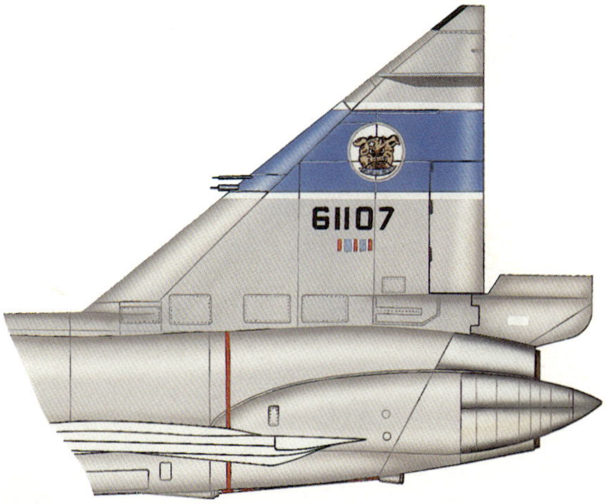
61107

NOV. 1964 - OCT. 1966

497th F.I.S.

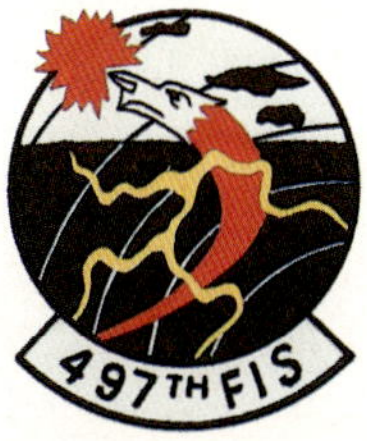
497TH FIS

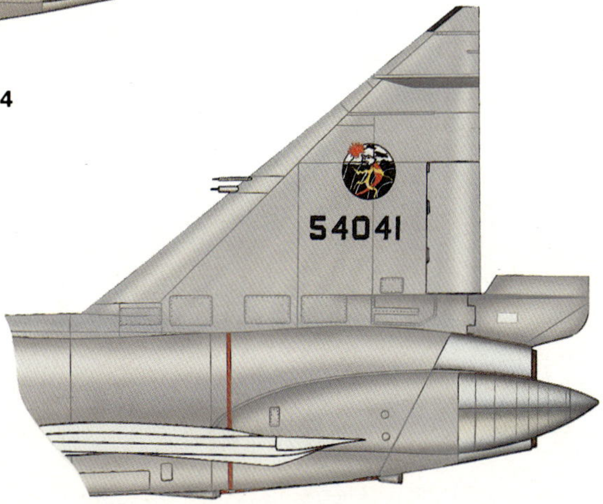
54041

EARLY 1961 - 1964

The national insignia on camouflaged F-102A Delta Daggers was far smaller than the insignia carried on the earlier Air Defense Command Gray aircraft. This was done to avoid compromising the camouflage effect. Later the insignia would be toned down by removing the colors. (Author)

This TF-102A carries the standard South East Asia camouflage scheme which consisted of Tan, Dark Green, and Medium Green uppersurfaces over Light Gray undersides. The aircraft was assigned to the 32nd FIS on 9 June 1969. (Author)

Not long after receiving camouflaged F-102A, the 32nd FIS was re-equipped and redesignated as a Tactical Fighter Squadron. The F-102s would be returned to the U.S. and issued to Air National Guard squadrons. (Author)

431st Fighter Interceptor Squadron

The 431st Fighter Interceptor Squadron operated in Spain out of Zaragoza Air Base as part of the USAF's contribution of fighter squadrons to the Spanish air defense system. Under the division of responsibilities, the squadron was assigned to the 65th Air Division and given the mission of air defense for north eastern Spain. On 22 June 1960, the 431st FIS sent twelve airmen to Torrejon Air Base, for a three week training course on the F-102. These men were followed by six pilots who began transition training during September of 1960.

The first F-102A was delivered to the squadron from Saint-Nazaire, France, by the unit commander, LTCOL Joseph J. McCabe on 28 September 1960. On 24 October, the squadron began its official transition to the F-102 and the unit was declared combat ready in late January 1961, reassuming its alert commitment on the 28th. The last of the twenty-nine Delta Daggers assigned to the unit arrived in Spain on 14 February 1961.

Along with the F-102As, two TF-102As were delivered to the squadron on a temporary basis: 55-4038 was delivered from the 497th FIS while 54-1367 was flown in from the 496th FIS. Both TF-102As were later reassigned to other USAFE units sometime before May of 1961. The unit also operated three T-33As.

The 431st deployed to Wheelus AB from 5 March until 28 April 1961 for weapons training with their new F-102s. The deployments consisted of four flights, each of which stayed for two weeks. The first two flights claimed a number of records and firsts during the deployment including: highest overall success rate for a single deployment, most consecutive successful intercepts in one day, highest number of aircraft with successful missile firings in a single day, highest number of pilots qualified in one day, and the most aircraft qualified in one day.

The unit returned to Wheelus from 26 May to 20 July 1962 to conduct simulated and live firings of AIM-26 missiles. By the end of July 1962, the 431st was certified to carry Falcons and as of 1 August, two AIM-26 loaded F-102As were standing one-hour alerts.

During the first half of 1962 the 431st FIS began sharing the alert hangar with Spanish Air Force F-86F Sabres of the 21st Fighter Squadron. During the Cuban missile crisis, half of the squadron's pilots and aircraft were on full alert from 22 Oct to 17 Nov 1962.

Early in 1962 degradation of the bearings, bushings, washers, and spacers in the flight control systems caused problems with eighteen TF/F-102As within the squadron. These were all older aircraft (FY54 and FY55 aircraft) and replacement of these items was included in the FY63 MOD/IRAN program.

A third deployment to Wheelus AB was undertaken from 6 July to 2 Aug 1963. Besides weapons training and live firing practice, the squadron also tested new intercept tactics for the USAFE Interceptor Weapons School. The new tactics involved a beam approach and a snap-up maneuver.

An F-102A-50-CO (55-3438) of the 431st FIS parked in the radar nose dock area at Zaragoza Air Base, Spain, during 1960. These single aircraft sheds were used to shelter technicians working on the aircraft's electronics. (431st FIS)

Awards

The 431st FIS was awarded the AF Outstanding Unit Award for the period 20 March 1961 to 9 February 1962 and several aircraft in the unit carried the award ribbon painted on the vertical fin below the serial number block.

Colors

During the squadron's early period, a number of aircraft carried a large squadron emblem on the plain Gray fin. The unit's highly distinctive tail markings, made up of a Satan's head and five Yellow stars against a Red band, was introduced during December of 1961. A2C Stephen Chianese designed the insignia and the first aircraft repainted with the marking was 56-1006, which also carried commander's stripes (three Red stripes on a White background).

The design was hand painted on all the unit's aircraft, which took a lot of time (two aircraft each weekend) since the flying schedule could not be disrupted. Airman Chianese was assisted by A2C Dan J. Hinchee and SSGT Billy A. Collins. As part of the original scheme, the intake boundary layer slabs and the braking parachute housings were also painted in flight colors. Red for A flight, Black for B flight, Blue for C flight and Green for D flight.

A tow bar has been attached to the nosewheel of this F-102A of the 431st FIS. The aircraft carries a commander's band around the fuselage consisting of three Red stripes. (USAF via S. Chianese)

An F-102A-25-CO (53-1818) of the 496th FIS parked on the ramp at Hahn Air Base, Germany during the early sixties. The aircraft in the background is a Military Air Transport Service (MATS) C-124 Globemaster. (D. Menard)

This F-102A-60-CO of the 525th FIS on the ramp at Bitburg Air Base, Germany, has the pilot's (LT Roberts, right) and crew chief's (A/1C Tillery, left) name painted on the Blue and Red Delta Dagger silhouettes on the nose. (Raymond Roberts)

A Red, White and Blue tailed F-102A-55-CO of the 32 FIS on the snow covered taxiway at Soesterberg Air Base, The Netherlands, during February of 1963. The aircraft has the squadron badge painted on the fin just above the serial number. (Author)

An F-102A-55-CO (56-1027) on the ramp at Kelly AFB, Texas, during June of 1960. The aircraft has finished its preparation for delivery to the port of embarkation (Brookley AFB) and shipment to Europe. (USAF Logistics Command)

An F-102A (56-1238) of the 526th Fighter Interceptor Squadron. The aircraft carries crew name F-102 silhouettes on the nose. (C. Snyder via D. Menard)

The Bulldog squadron emblem of the 525th FIS was carried on a White circle on the vertical stabilizer above the serial number block. The White containers behind the crewmen are weapons shipping containers for Falcon air-to-air missiles. (Raymond Roberts)

An F-102A-LO (56-1111) of the 525th FIS on the ramp at RAF Wethersfield, England, on 17 June 1961. The aircraft carries the unit emblem on the fin just above the serial number block. (G. Pennick)

This F-102A-60-CO (56-1086) of the 525th FIS on the taxiway at Soesterberg Air Base, The Netherlands, on 16 August 1965 has an Air Force Outstanding Unit Award ribbon painted on the fin below the serial number. (A.G. v.d. Brink)

This F-102A carries the unit's highly visible insignia on the fin. The young man on the right is Stephen Chianese who designed the scheme and did the painting on the aircraft assisted by Billy Collins (middle) and Dan Hinchee. (USAF via S. Chianese)

An F-102A (56-0983) of the 431st FIS breaks away after completing visual identification of the target over the Mediterranean Sea during early 1962. The F-102s were required to close to within visual range of their target to get a positive identification. (USAF via S. Chianese)

It is certain that the tail art was painted on all aircraft; however; the intake slabs and brake 'chute housing were not done at the same time and a number of aircraft were unpainted.

At sometime during their operational career with the squadron, the sidewalls of the tires were painted White. The two TF-102As were given considerably larger tail markings so that they could be easily identified. The tail markings were retained until the unit retired the F-102s, and about half of the aircraft still had the tail markings in place when they were ferried back to the U.S. during 1964.

Accidents

On 3 May 1961 the unit's forty-three month record of accident-free flying ended when material failure on F-102A 55-3434 led to damage to three other F-102s on the squadron's ramp at Zaragoza. The aircraft was ready to taxi when an explosion damaged the throttle linkage causing the engine to accelerate. After a high speed spiral around the ramp, the aircraft came to rest after striking TF-102A 54-1367 and two F-102As (55-3431 and 56-0975). All four aircraft were repaired by CASA, but were out of service for a long time.

On 8 September 1961, TF-102A 55-4038 crashed into the Mediterranean Sea off Barcelona. The squadron commander, LTCOL Joseph J. McCabe, was drowned after he and his co-pilot successfully ejected. The co-pilot was rescued by a Navy helicopter.

On 11 June 1962, F-102A 55-3451 suffered a mishap at Zaragoza AB. On a takeoff roll, the left main landing gear strut failed, causing the aircraft to veer off the left side of the runway. The damage was confined mainly to the left wing and belly and it was repaired by the CASA factory at Madrid (the repairs were completed early in 1964).

Another accident took place on 12 December 1963 when F-102A 56-1012 crashed some fifty miles from Zaragoza AB. 1st LT Joseph L. Higgins had an engine flameout at 35,000 feet during a routine mission and could not relight the engine. After gliding down to 8,000 feet, he ejected and was picked up uninjured some twenty minutes later by a helicopter. Two other F-102s were flying with Higgins at the time of the incident. CAPT Robert C. Solomon watched Higgins descend in his parachute and reported his position to the rescue helicopter, while CAPT Henry K. Mills followed the pilotless aircraft.

The F-102A suddenly turned toward a cluster of small towns and it quickly became evident that the aircraft might crash among the three villages. CAPT Mills maneuvered his aircraft close to and below the F-102A so that the flow of air over his wing raised the wing of "012," turning it away from the populated area. When the crippled aircraft turned too far, CAPT Mills repeated the maneuver on the other side until the aircraft finally crashed landed harmlessly into a ploughed field.

An F-102A of the 431st Fighter Interceptor Squadron flies over the Mediterranean Sea off the coast of Spain during early 1962. Most of the intercepts flown by the 431st took place over water. (S. Chianese)

Two TF-102As lead a lineup of F-102A Delta Daggers of the 431st FIS on the ramp at Zaragoza Air Base, Spain, during 1963. The small vehicle alongside the TF-102 is an electrical generator used to provide the aircraft with ground power. (USAF)

Phase Out

On 13 November 1963, the 431st FIS received an order to plan for the unit's disbandment and on 1 March 1964 the unit was relieved of its alert commitment. On 30 March the squadron was ordered to discontinue operations on or about 18 May 1964. This order was rescinded on 16 July and on 25 July the unit was redesignated as the 431st Tactical Fighter Squadron and assigned to the 8th TFW, flying F-4C Phantoms.

Most of the F-102s were ferried to the U.S. between 15 April and 1 June 1964. The last aircraft to leave was TF-102A (55-4045) which left Zaragoza on 23 April 1964.

Postscript

Personnel of the 431st Test and Evaluation Squadron (TAC), the 406th CLSS, the 2951st CLSS at McClellan AFB, California, together with Museum volunteers and an Aircraft Paint Unit, rebuilt an F-102A (56-1140) and repainted it to represent aircraft (5-5431). The restoration was completed during 1985 and the aircraft was presented to the McClellan AFB Museum on 13 January 1986. The aircraft was painted with the Red devil tail markings used by the squadron in Spain and was officially dedicated to the memory of LTCOL McCabe (killed in a crash on 8 September 1961).

This TF-102A-20-CO of the 431st FIS has the U.S. AIR FORCE and Buzz number, TC-367, painted on the fuselage in the wrong order. The aircraft was visiting Soesterberg Air Base in The Netherlands on 2 July 1963. (Author)

This TF-102A (55-4045) of the 431st FIS was visiting Soesterberg Air Base, The Netherlands, on 10 March 1964. The tips of the underwing fuel tanks are painted Red. TF-102As were used to conduct navigational training and were frequent visitors. (Author)

An F-102A of the 431st FIS on the taxiway at Prestwick, Scotland, on 15 April 1964. The aircraft was being ferried back to the U.S. The upper portion of the braking parachute housing is White. (MAP)

These F-102As (56-1227 and 56-1260) of the 526th FIS on takeoff from Ramstein AB, Germany, during December of 1964, reveal a variety of markings. Aircraft 227 has the squadron emblem on the fin without the fin band, while 260 has the unit emblem painted over the band. (Emory Kristof/National Geographic)

An F-102A-70-CO (56-1235) of the 526th Fighter Interceptor Squadron is admired by a British airman. The inside of the braking parachute housing is painted in Chromate Green. (C. Snyder via D. Menard)

Late in their European careers most F-102As were repainted in Southeast Asia camouflage. The camouflage consists of Tan, Medium Green and Dark Green uppersurfaces over Light Gray undersurfaces. (Larry Davis)

496th Fighter Interceptor Squadron

The 496th Fighter Interceptor Squadron exchanged their worn and weary F-86D Sabres for supersonic F-102s during the Fall of 1959. While squadron personnel underwent F-102 transition training, the runway at Hahn Air Base, Germany, was closed for reconstruction work (lasting until December 1959).

On 9 December 1959, two F-102As (53-1809, 54-1402) and two TF-102As (55-4059, 56-2329) landed at Hahn. These were the first of twenty-six aircraft slated for the squadron. The first F-102 landing at Hahn was made by MAJ Francis Lawson, the squadron operations officer. While aircraft were still being delivered from France, the squadron deployed a number of aircraft to Wheelus AB for weapons training on 18 January 1960. The unit deployed small groups of Daggers until 10 March 1960.

Twenty-one F-102As again deployed to Wheelus Air Base for weapons training from 2 Aug until 22 Aug 1960 and all aircraft except one successfully checked out with the WSEM. During this period, live missile firings were conducted and sixty-five percent of the squadron aircraft were qualified.

Between March and July of 1960, the squadron's aircraft were all involved in a local modification program conducted at Hahn. The radar equipment was brought up to the FIG-6 configuration by technicians from the FIAT Aircraft Corp., of Torino, Italy. On 8 December 1960 the squadron's aircraft started the FIG-7 modification program.

During 1960, the squadron requested a new unit insignia, since it was felt that the old insignia represented the F-86D. The new insignia, a gauntleted hand with a White Falcon, was officially approved on 2 September 1960. During 1964, the insignia was slightly changed, with the color of the Falcon being changed to Brown (this change was not officially approved).

During 1961 and 1962, several F-102s from other units were temporararily assigned to the squadron while a number of their aircraft underwent modification by field technicians. The runway at Hahn AB was resurfaced during 1960, 1961, 1962 and 1963 which resulted in deploying aircraft to Ramstein Air Base and/or Bitburg Air Base for several weeks each time.

During 1964 the squadron made several deployments to other German airfields and to Torrejon Air Base, Spain. The winter weather in Central Europe was usually bad with low ceilings, fog and snow. Torrejon allowed a good alternative for flight training and the first deployment was made from 28 November 1964 until 30 January 1965. An average of six aircraft were usually deployed to Spain. During these deployments both pilots and aircraft were rotated between Hahn and Torrejon. These deployments were very successful because all the squadron's "low time pilots" were able to build up flying time. Additionally, a number of low level intercepts, both over water and over land were successfully conducted.

From 6 March until 24 June 1964, the 496th FIS received twenty-three newer aircraft, twenty of which came from the 497th FIS. This

The large F-102 silhouettes on the nose of this F-102A-40-CO (54-1402) of the 496th Fighter Interceptor Squadron were used to display the pilot's and crew chief's name. These were common on USAFE F-102s during the mid-1960s.

trade was requested by the commander of the 86th AD. The older F-102s were returned to the U.S. under Operation KRAZY KAT.

The 496th also deployed flights of aircraft to the south of Germany for exercise purposes. Erding Air Base hosted F-102As from Hahn AB for the first time during July of 1966, while another deployment took place during 1966 (October). There were three exercise deployments during 1967 (March, July and October/November). During 1968, there were two such exercises (February and April) and lastly during 1969 the squadron went to Erding during February/March.

On 19 Aug 1966, the squadron registered a first when the first field arrested landing was made using the field arrestor hook on the F-102. With no margin for error, a relatively new pilot (ninety-five F-102 hours), LT Frank Furr, made a successful arrestment after a tire blew on takeoff. He circled and prepared for the landing while the base fire department sprayed down a coating of foam on the runway, minimizing the possibility of sparks and a fire.

Awards

The 496th FIS shared the Air Force Outstanding Unit Award given to the 86th Air Division for the period 1 July 1964 to 30 June 1965.

During 1968, the 496th won the Huddleston Trophy (together with JG-74 of the West German Air Force) for the 1968 AFCENT Air Defense Competition. It represented Sector 3, which won the first place sector award.

Three F-102As of the 496th FIS sit on the rain soaked ramp at Wheelus Air Base. The color of the fin markings was Yellow and Black, while the background for the serial number block was in Air Defense Command Gray. (Chuck Downing)

This F-102A (53-1801) of the 496th FIS has a Red rotating beacon on the upper fuselage spine which was introduced as a modification during 1964. The aircraft also carries pilot/crew chief markings on the nose.

A pilot climbs into the cockpit of an F-102A (54-1399) of the 496th FIS on the ramp at Prestwick, Scotland, on 15 April 1964. The aircraft was being returned to the U.S. and stopped in Prestwick for fuel. (MAP)

Colors

During early May of 1960, the sunburst tail markings were introduced on F-102 54-1405, which was also painted with commander's special markings consisting of a Black and Yellow band around the nose section. During 1961 the squadron added two F-102 silhouettes on the port side of the nose which were retained up to the Spring of 1964.

During July of 1964, the 496th became the first unit in the 86th AD to introduce the colored band on the fin in Yellow (the squadron color). Additionally, the 496th was the only unit to add stars on the tail band. The insignias of both the 496th and the 86th were added to the band and the braking parachute housing was painted in Black and Yellow.

Sometime during 1964-1966 a number of aircraft were given colored nosewheel doors (Blue, Red or Yellow). A number of others carried a Yellow flash (outlined in Black) on the underwing drop tanks. The unit commander's aircraft (56-1080) was painted with a Black-Yellow-Red band around the fuselage just behind the cockpit.

During November of 1966, the first camouflaged aircraft were taken on strength. The first aircraft was TF-102A (54-1366) which was delivered on 8 November 1965. The last squadron aircraft to be repainted was F-102A 56-1384 on 7 March 1968.

Accidents

The unit was unfortunate in that it had the highest number of F-102s lost (six) and damaged (five) in USAFE.

Ground crews do routine maintenance around an F-102A (54-1406) of the 496th FIS. This aircraft has all the FIG-8 modifications including the infrared scanner on the nose and the field arresting hook. (MAP)

On 20 July 1960, F-102A 53-1818 crashed some twenty-five miles from Ramstein AB, Germany, after a severe compressor stall. The pilot successfully ejected. On 22 August 1960, F-102A 54-1378 crashed in France on its return flight from Wheelus AB. The pilot had reported control problems but remained with his aircraft. He was fatally injured in the crash.

On 22 November 1961, F-102A 54-1375 was damaged beyond repair by a fire in the rear section. A fourth F-102A (54-1404) crashed on 24 January 1964 about fifty miles from Hahn AB. During a practice intercept at 35,000 feet, the aircraft flamed out and the pilot was unable to obtain a relight.

On 17 May 1966, aircraft 56-1090 crashed five miles SE of Pforzheim, Germany. On 16 February 1967, F-102A 56-1045 crashed nine miles Northeast of Hahn AB. It was on final approach to Hahn with intermittent radio difficulties. The pilot elected to make a formation GCA recovery with his flight leader. The gear was lowered and the speed brakes extended when the aircraft began a gentle but uncontrollable roll to the left. With less than 1,000 feet remaining, the pilot successfully ejected. The aircraft was replaced by one sent over from the U.S. (56-1384).

On 11 February 1961, aircraft 54-1399 was involved in an accident at Ramstein AB. The aircraft was given temporary repairs and was then flown to Chateauroux Air Base, France, for additional repairs. The aircraft did not return to the unit until 2 June 1962.

On 3 March 1964, F-102A 53-1810 was scrambled on an early morning mission. Due to fog at Hahn AB, the flight was diverted to Bitburg after the mission, where the weather was at minimums. The pilot was unable to extend the nosewheel and he was advised to make an approach end BAK-9 barrier engagement. The landing cracked the fuselage at the forward electronics compartment. It was repaired at Bitburg AB by a team sent in from the San Antonio AMA and returned to the U.S. on 1 June 1964.

On 15 July 1964, 56-1121 landed at Hahn AB with damage after a mid-air collision with a West German Air Force Dornier Do-27B. In the mid-air, the Delta Dagger struck the light aircraft, cutting off a large part of the Do-27's right wing. The Dornier crashed, killing both crew members.

F-102A 56-1099 made an emergency landing at Stuttgart Airport, Germany, on 29 Aug 1968 and was repaired a month later. This aircraft had suffered electrical problems while on a mission and the pilot declared an emergency to the civil tower. He was cleared to land and made a steep final approach. He had excessive approach

The commander's band on this F-102A of the 496th FIS is unusual. It is much wider than normal and consists of Yellow and Black stripes separated by thin White stripes.

A Southeast Asia camouflaged F-102A (56-1080) of the 496th FIS on the taxiway at Soesterberg Air Base on 15 August 1968. The national insignia is much smaller than on the earlier ADC Gray painted aircraft.

During the transition from the ADC Gray aircraft to the camouflage scheme, it was not uncommon for aircraft in both color schemes to operate together like this pair of F-102As of the 496th FIS during early 1966. (Author)

speed and performed an "S" turn in an attempt to lose both altitude and airspeed. The aircraft touched down 2,100 feet from the approach end of the runway at 170 knots. After approximately 100 feet, both main wheels locked and the tires blew. The aircraft finally ran off the runway at the 7,500 foot marker and came to rest twenty feet off the right side of the runway.

The last Squadron mishap occurred at Hahn on 1 August 1969 and involved aircraft 56-1053.

Phase Out

From October until December 1969 the squadron sent several F-102 pilots for F-4E Phantom training in the U.S. in preparation for unit conversion to the Phantom. On 1 January 1970, the 496th was redesignated a Tactical Fighter Squadron. After a ten year stay as Hahn's guardians, the twenty-two F-102s departed Hahn.

The F-102As were flown by ANG pilots of the 194th FIS, California Air National Guard, the squadron which received the aircraft. One aircraft (56-1121) had the ANG insignia applied to the fin before it left Hahn AB. The squadron's two TF-102As were flown to the U.S. by regular Air Force pilots. The first F-4E Phantoms landed at Hahn on 10 February 1970, ending the F-102 era.

An F-102A of the 496th FIS on final approach for landing at Hahn Air Base, Germany, on 10 August 1966. The aircraft has the 86th Air Division insignia on the fin band, and the drag 'chute housing is in Yellow and Black. (Author)

A camouflaged F-102A (56-1082) of the 496th FIS chocked on the ramp at RAF Lakenheath, England, on 11 May 1968. The aircraft has the new style of serial placement on the fin along with the USAF legend in small Black letters.

497th Fighter Interceptor Squadron

The 497th began its relationship with the F-102 during early 1960 when the unit's F-86D flight simulator was replaced by an F-102 simulator. During April of 1960, six pilots who already had some experience with F-102s were sent to Bitburg AB, Germany, for transition training. Upon return, these pilots acted as instructors for the rest of the squadron.

On 26 April 1960, the unit's first F-102A (56-1136) landed at Torrejon after its delivery flight from France. The aircraft was piloted by COL Clay Tice Jr., commander of the 65th AD. The remaining twenty-five aircraft were delivered over the next three months with the last arriving on 13 July 1960.

The number of F-86Ds was gradually reduced with three Sabres being withdrawn each week. By the end of March 1960, all the F-86Ds had been retired. On 1 May the 497th was relieved of its alert commitment to complete transition to the F-102s. By 1 August the unit had completed transition and combat crew training and, after a deployment of all its F-102s to Wheelus AB for weapons proficiency training (22 August to 10 September 1960), the pilots of the 497th were declared operationally ready in the Delta Dagger.

The squadron assumed air defense alert on 14 September 1960 and on 1 April 1962 the 497th deployed six aircraft to Wheelus AB for two weeks of weapons training and live missile firing. By 26 May, the entire squadron had rotated through Wheelus AB.

During the 1962 deployment, one flight set a new record at the Wheelus range. Some 84.3 percent of high altitude intercepts were successfully completed, while 87.7 percent of all low altitude intercepts were completed.

During August of 1961, the 497th was notified that it was to represent USAFE in the William Tell Tournament at Tyndall AFB, Florida, during October. In the event, the world situation did not permit the participation of overseas squadrons in the meet.

This TF-102A (55-4041) of the 497th FIS has the Air Force Outstanding Unit Award ribbon painted on the fin just ahead of the serial number block. The aircraft also had the squadron name lettered on the underwing drop tanks.

Awards

One of the unit's officers received a "Well Done" award during May of 1962. CAPT Nathaniel O. Devoll was praised for his high degree of ability and professionalism in saving a F-102 from damage or loss. CAPT Devoll was on initial approach to Wheelus Air Base at 1,500 feet (three miles from the approach end) when the engine flamed out. Immediately, he attempted a "relight" first using the emergency system, then the normal system. Neither worked. CAPT Devoll declared an emergency and, holding off on extending his gear and speed brakes until the runway was assured, smoothly executed a dead-stick landing.

The 497th FIS was a runner-up for the coveted "Hughes Trophy" during 1961 and 1962, and won it in 1963. In August of 1961, the 497th was chosen as the recipient of the 65th Air Division Award for the "Outstanding Fighter Interceptor Squadron" (1 January through 30 June 1961).

During 1962 the 497th received the "Air Force Outstanding Unit Award" for the period 20 March 1961 to 9 February 1962 and the squadron's two TF-102As were painted with the chevron on the fin.

Colors

While the aircraft carried no unit markings while in Spain, some retained a part of the markings of their earlier squadron, the 82nd FIS. A number of aircraft later carried a large squadron emblem on both sides of the fin.

Accidents

The squadron has a remarkable safety record with none of its F-102s being lost, although one was damaged. 56-1121 was damaged at Torrejon on 2 October 1961. It received temporary repairs and was flown to Chateauroux AB, France, for overhaul. The aircraft returned to the squadron on 18 June 1962.

One minor incident involved a Spanish flight surgeon, CAPT Luis de la Serna. He had been invited to take a supersonic ride in a TF-102A by LTCOL George Halliwell, commander of the 497th. For the first part of the orientation flight everything went smoothly, but when near the speed of sound at 33,000 feet, half of the windshield

Flight crews scramble to their aircraft during an alert at Torrejon Air Base, Spain, during 1963. The F-102s of the 497th FIS operated alongside F-86Fs of the 61st Fighter Squadron, Spanish Air Force.(USAF)

A TF-102A (56-2331) lands at Bitburg AB, Germany, on 28 January 1959 after a delivery flight from Saint-Nazaire, France. The aircraft still has the Arctic Red fin of its former unit, the Alaskan Air Command. (USAF)

shattered. Emergency procedures were started and LCOL. Halliwell instructed his passenger to prepare for a possible ejection. Since the cockpit was pressurized, the pressure had to be released in order to reduce the chances of the glass blowing out. The aircraft headed back to Torrejon and made a successful emergency landing with both the glass and the passenger intact.

Phase Out

On 25 July 1964, the squadron was redesignated a Tactical Fighter Squadron and was assigned to the 8th TFW at George AFB, flying the F-4C Phantom II. The entire inventory of F-102As were reassigned to other European squadrons, although the two TF-102As were returned to the U.S.

The last F-102A (56-1062) left Torrejon on 3 June 1964, destined for Hahn Air Base, in Germany.

A flight of four Delta Daggers of the 525th FIS stationed at Bitburg Air Base, Germany, during early 1959. Two of the aircraft still carry the Red tail markings of their former unit, the 317th FIS in Alaska. (USAF)

525th Fighter Interceptor Squadron

The 525th FIS began transition training from the F-86D to the F-102A at its home base of Bitburg, Germany. A number of experienced F-102 pilots were sent to Bitburg during late 1958 to start both the ground school and to conduct flight training. They were assisted by a number of factory representatives who helped train maintenance personnel.

The 525th FIS was the first European squadron to transition to the Delta Dagger and on 28 January 1959 they took position of their first aircraft when a TF-102A (56-2331), flown by MAJ Barnard H. Barton, touched down at Bitburg. He was in the lead of a flight of two TF-102As and three F-102As, the first of some twenty-five aircraft that would be delivered to the squadron (the last arrived on 7 March 1959).

In March of 1960, the Link Division of General Precision, Inc. delivered and installed an F-102 flight simulator to assist with F-102 conversion training for new pilots and for navigation/instrument training for all the squadron's pilots.

Despite having just reached operational status, the 525th participated in the 1959 William Tell Weapons Competition at Tyndall AFB, Florida. To everyone's surprise, the squadron took the lead

F-102As of the 525th FIS on the ramp at Bitburg Air Base, Germany, during the early 1960s. The crew name F-102 silhouettes were not used on all the squadron's aircraft at this time. (USAF via L. Prichard)

The two F-102 markings on the nose of this F-102A of the 525th FIS are Blue with Red flames and White lettering. The upper marking has the pilot's name while the lower one has the crew chief's name on the body and the assistant crew chief's name on the flame. (Raymond D. Roberts)

and kept it until the last mission. Upon landing after the last sortie, they found that they had been nosed out by the 460th FIS by a very narrow margin. The team captain was the commander of the 86th TFW, COL Robert J. Rogers.

The 525th made several deployments to Wheelus AB for weapons training and live missile firing exercises. Four F-102As deployed to Wheelus from 13 to 29 July 1959, with a second deployment being made by some twenty-three F-102As from 19 November to 20 December. During the Wheelus deployments, the unit's TF-102As remained at Bitburg.

The weapons training included intensive training on the over water firing range, where a number of live missile launches were made by each pilot, greatly increasing their combat proficiency. In these missile exercises, the GAR-1D radar controlled version of the Falcon air-to-air missile was used. These were the first such firing exercises with the Falcon at Wheelus, and the first in USAFE. The missiles were fired at DELMAR radar targets, towed by B-57 aircraft at the end of a four mile long cable.

Before each pilot actually fired a live missile, he flew three pre-firing practice runs. These sorties were recorded on tape so that the training officers could study the pilot's performance. The tape would show if he had thrown all the proper switches to activate the weapons system and if he had flown the correct approach to the target. After completing his first F-102 live firing mission over the Mediterranean range, LTCOL Charles W. Carson Jr., commander of the 525th FIS, stated that he was impressed by the "vastly improved intercept capability" represented by the combination of the F-102 and Falcon.

Between 16 March and 14 July 1960, the FIAT Aircraft Corporation of Torino, Italy, sent a team of technicians and installers to bring the radar equipment on all the 525th's aircraft up to the FIG-6 configuration. This was followed some five months later by a program to further update the aircraft to the FIG-7 configuration. This modification program was conducted at Chateauroux Air Base, France, with the first aircraft departing Bitburg on 1 December 1960.

During a one-week training deployment to Wheelus Air Base (7-14 September 1962) B flight set a new range record of an eighty percent success rate in radar intercepts against high altitude targets. The radar reflective DELMAR targets were towed by F-100 Super Sabres at altitudes over 40,000 feet. For low altitude intercepts, T-33As were fitted with radar reflectors and flown at very low level (500 feet). B flight successful completed fifty-two out of sixty-five "hot" runs (missiles fired) and "dry" WSEM qualification runs over a gruelling six day period. This beat the next nearest one-week deployment effort for F-102s by some eight percent.

The last day of the exercise, B flight set a sixteen for sixteen successful intercepts, beating the former record (525th FIS) of eleven out of eleven by a wide margin. The deployment was led by LTCOL James M. Thomas, the squadron commander, and CAPT Thomas J. Wicker served as B Flight leader.

This F-102A (56-1060) of the 525th FIS crashed on a hilltop in Germany on 18 June 1961. The holes in the rear fuselage were probably caused by turbine blades from the engine. (USAF)

A ground crewman plugs a fuel hose into an F-102A (56-1265) of the 525th FIS on the ramp at Bitburg Air Base, Germany, on 3 October 1961. The F-102 burned JP-4 jet fuel. (USAF)

An F-102A-60-Co (56-1120) 525th FIS, flies over Germany during October of 1963. The F-102s represented the state-of-the-art in all-weather interceptors during the early 1960s. (Quadrant Picture Library)

One of the unit's TF-102As (56-2331) set a European record for flying hours within a month, when it flew seventy-one hours thirty-five minutes during March 1962. Of the thirty-five sorties flown by 56-2331, twenty-five required no maintenance follow-ups and no discrepancies were logged. The unit's two seat Dagger was flown more than the average F-102A because it was used to train new pilots and to conduct instrument check rides for all squadron pilots.

A 525th FIS pilot made the first successful field arrested landing with an F-102 on 23 July 1963. CAPT Leslie J. Prichard had the port main tire on his F-102 blow on takeoff nearly causing a collision with his wingman. The two Delta Daggers were now safely airborne, but to save the damaged F-102A, the squadron operation officer, LTCOL Robert L. Embary, decided to order the pilot to make an arrested landing.

A five mile straight-in approach was set up, with the gear down, speed brakes out and arrestor hook extended. CAPT Prichard established a fairly flat, power on approach and made his touchdown 1,100 feet from the arresting gear. The braking parachute was deployed immediately to help slow the aircraft and the nosewheel steering system was engaged. The blown tire caused the F-102 to vibrate so violently that a hydraulic line ruptured causing the port brake to fail. By using the starboard brake, CAPT Prichard was able to maintain some directional control. The drag chute was lost just prior to engaging the arresting gear, which brought the aircraft to a smooth and safe stop without further damage.

Competitions and Awards

The 525 FIS "Bulldogs" won the 86th Air Division Commander's Trophy three times: May and November of 1960 and 25 May 1961. This quarterly award was known as the "Most Effective Squadron" trophy and had been initiated during the Autumn of 1959. The 525th received these award for accomplishments in training, exercises, operational readiness and flying hours.

The 525th represented USAFE in the "F-102 World Wide Loading Conference," held at Seymour Johnson AFB during September of 1962. This ten-day event was attended by representatives from PACAF, Alaskan Air Command, Air Defense Command and USAFE. The teams competed for points given for speed and efficiency

The canopy has been blown off this F-102A (56-1253) of the 525th FIS after it suffered a landing accident at Bitburg Air Base, Germany, on 3 January 1961. More than likely, the canopy was jettisoned by the rescue personnel. (USAF)

This F-102A (56-1479) was a loaned aircraft used by the 525th FIS during the 1959 William Tell Weapons Meet. The painting on the fin was carried by the Delta Dagger only for the duration of the meet. (USAF)

The F-102 usually landed in a nose high attitude like this F-102A (56-1076) of the 525th FIS landing at Bitburg Air Base, Germany. The fin colors were Blue and White. (USAF via L. Prichard)

in missile rail inspections, aircraft weapons system condition and serviceability, electrical checks performed on all missile rails, missile inspections, missile loading, missile arming and finally retraction of the loaded launchers and closing of the missile bay doors. The five-man team from the 525th had been accepted by the USAFE during drills held at Ramstein AB during which all 86th AD F-102 teams completed. An average F-102 loading speed was fifteen minutes, but the is team completed it's tasks in an 8 1/2 minute average.

The 525th won the USAFE "Little Willy Tell" competition, held between the 525th and 497th Fighter Interceptor Squadrons on 5 July 1963, and was picked to represent USAFE at the 1963 "William Tell Fighter Weapons Meet" held from 7 to 14 October 1963. The squadron borrowed aircraft from units in the U.S. which led to numerous difficulties, especially in the radars and missile bays.

These malfunctions had to be corrected before the flying program could begin and further problems occurred during the competition. On the first mission, the lead aircraft had an ignitor cable disconnect in flight, resulting in a misfire of the missile. On another mission the number three aircraft blew a fuse in the fire control system just before the missiles fired, resulting in a failure of the missiles to guide. In two other cases missiles failed to guide for unknown reasons. As a result of these problems, the 525th placing fourth in the F-102 category.

On 23 May 1964 the unit received the Air Force Outstanding Unit Award for the period 1 January 1962 to 31 December 1963. The squadron was presented this award because of its high aircraft in-commission rate, accuracy in missile firings, selection for participa-

The angled device behind this F-102A (56-1243) of the 525th FIS on the Bitburg ramp during the Summer of 1960 is a metal Jet Blast Deflector (JBD). These were common on NATO bases throughout Europe. (Raymond D. Roberts)

tion in "William Tell" and for the outstanding tactical evaluations the unit had received from USAFE and the 86th AD. During the period covered by the award, the squadron has also logged 14,508 accident-free flying hours.

The 525th FIS participated in all the USAFE/LOADEO Competitions held between 1965 and 1969. They won the competition in August of 1965, August of 1966 and August of 1969.

During 1968 the unit received the 86th Air Division Outstanding Unit Award. Finally, one 525th pilot achieved note when he became the first USAFE F-102 pilot to reach 1,000 hours in the Delta Dagger. CAPT Garry L. Tresemer, the squadron Tactical Evaluation Officer, reached this milestone during January of 1962.

Colors

The squadron originally gained a number of aircraft from the Alaskan Air Command and these were received still carrying the Artic Red fin and wingtips. These were repainted in Air Defense Command Gray as time allowed. Squadron insignias were added to both sides of the fin during May of 1959. A year later the sunburst tail markings of the 86th AD were introduced, with most aircraft carrying the squadron insignia on both sides of the fin as well. The Delta Dagger silhouettes were introduced during May of 1959 and continued in use until early 1964.

During 1960 aircraft 56-1264 was painted as the unit commander's aircraft with a Red-Yellow-Blue-Green-Yellow-Red band being applied to the fuselage just behind the cockpit. The sunburst tail markings were removed from the fin beginning in October of 1963, although some aircraft retained the markings until the Spring of 1964.

During 1964 the 86th Air Division insignia was applied to the starboard side of the fin along with the AF Outstanding Unit Award

ribbon. Additionally, the braking parachute housing was painted in flight colors (Red, White or Blue).

During October of 1964 the aircraft received a horizontal Blue band on the fin. The first aircraft to be painted in the new markings was the unit's TF-102A (56-2333). F-102A 56-1044 was painted as the commander's aircraft with a band going around the fuselage consisting of three Blue and Four white stripes.

The first European F-102 to be painted in SEA camouflage was assigned to the 525th. The F-102A (56-1214) returned to Bitburg AB from the CASA factories on 19 October 1965 carrying the new colors. By the end of 1967, eighteen aircraft had been camouflaged, the last being 56-1512 on 16 April 1968.

Aircraft Accidents

During July of 1960, the 525th FIS set a safety record for accident free flying with the F-102. During the fifteen months since the unit re-equipped with the F-102, none of its pilots had been involved in an aircraft accident.

This record could not continue forever and, on 26 November 1960, an F-102A (56-1243) was lost at Bitburg. On that morning the F-102 departed from the alert hangar on a scramble. The pilot hit his afterburner and raised the landing gear lever (normally, this allowed the gear to retract as soon as the aircraft's weight was off of them). This time, however, it retracted immediately. The F-102 travelled about half way down the runway on its belly with afterburner engaged. The result was that the belly was totally torn off the aircraft (although the pilot was uninjured).

On 18 June 1961, aircraft 56-1060 crashed between Badern and Erdorf, some five miles from Hahn AB. The pilot, LTCOL John B. Anderson, commander of the 525th, successfully ejected. He had been attempting to land the aircraft at night, in bad weather, after suffering a primary hydraulic system failure. He made several approaches without ever sighting the airfield and finally decided to eject. The pilotless aircraft circled three times and crashed into an open field. After the impact, a flash fire occurred destroying the aircraft.

Another loss near the home base occurred on 18 Oct 1964 when 56-1178 had an inflight fire which destroyed the flight control sys-

Ground crews dismantle a crashed F-102A (56-1060) of the 525th FIS during June of 1961. The aircraft was completely taken apart and trucked back to the base so that an investigation might reveal the cause of the accident. (USAF)

tem. The pilot successfully bailed out and the aircraft crashed near Bitburg.

The squadron suffered three other losses: aircraft 56-1120 burned out at Bitburg on 8 November 1965; 56-1071 crashed twelve miles from Bernkastel, Germany, on 14 December 1965; and 56-1214 was lost in a landing accident at Spangdahlem Air Base on 13 May 1966. The wreck could still be seen beside the runway at least until the Summer of 1970.

A number of incidents also occurred to squadron aircraft. On 20 April 1959, 1st LT Raymond D. Roberts had a mishap flying an F-102. He later recalled that;

> *"I had a 90 degree hard turn on the nose wheel steering system when I let the nose down. When the nosewheel touched, the bird skidded some 90 degrees, left the runway, hit a marker sign, broke off the left main landing gear which caused other minor damage to the wing."*

This same pilot later received a USAFE Flying Safety Award during February 1960 for remaining with his aircraft after it experienced a serious control malfunction over Wiesbaden. Roberts remem-

The nose of this crashed F-102 has been covered with a tarp to protect the radar from further damage. With luck, some of the components might be salvaged for use as spare parts. (USAF)

This F-102A (56-1242) of the 525th Fighter Interceptor Squadron has a Blue breaking parachute housing. The aircraft was visiting Soesterberg Air Base, The Netherlands, on 20 March 1964. (Author)

bered the flight:

"It was a five AM flight. I started having severe flight control problems at 38,000 feet which I found were caused by the unequal cooling of hydraulic fluids and unequal expansion of parts in the hydraulic HEP valve. This caused the valve to work against itself and the flight controls started to move rapidly in all directions. As a result, I found myself going almost straight down with a severe porpoise, severe enough that I could not eject. It had me pinned to the top of the canopy with the seat belt down around my knees."

The aircraft recovered somewhat at 14,000 feet and after struggling with the controls for over an hour, Roberts managed to land at Bitburg AB.

56-1253 was damaged in an unusual accident at Bitburg AB on 3 January 1961. Snow had been pushed over to the side of the touchdown point and had became a frozen mountain. While landing, the F-102 drifted and struck the snow bank with its left main gear. The gear was ripped off and when the aircraft touched down, it immediately made a 60 degree turn off the runway, crossed a muddy field, tore out the boundary fence around the air base and lost the nosewheel. It took six months to repair the damage.

One highly unusual problem was encountered during December of 1961 by CAPT Thomas E. Wolters. After completing a normal flight, he landed at Ramstein and after taxiing off the runway toward the control tower, his brakes failed. He could not shut off the engine because he would lose his steering power.

He was rolling down the taxiway at a good clip with no way of stopping. He alerted the tower and the tower, in turn, informed all aircraft in the area that they had a runaway F-102. His first encounter was with an F-104 parked sideways across the taxiway — he avoided it by turning onto a parking ramp. After the F-104 was moved, Wolters turned back out into the taxiway. His next obstacle was another F-102. Wolters frantically waved and signaled to the other pilot to get out of the way. As he turned from the taxiway to the runway, he noticed he was being chased by a truck whose occupants were trying to figure out a way to stop the runaway craft.

Finally as he rolled down the runway, he realized he could stop the aircraft with his arrestor hook. He engaged the barrier and the aircraft finally came to a stop. A crazy ending to a routine flight.

Phase Out

On 1 October 1969 the 525th was renamed a Tactical Fighter Squadron and on 17 October the first group of twelve F-102s began their journey back to the U.S. under project CORNET EAST 35. The next day another eight Daggers left Bitburg, followed by the last two on 21 October 1969. Interviewed on the eve of their departure the squadron commander, LTCOL Thomas E. Wolters said:

"We all hate to see the old birds go. They fly just as well, or better, now than when we first got them. Some of these aircraft have flown from this base for eleven years. Some have more than 3,000 flying hours on them, but when the Air Guard units get them, they will be ready to go."

An F-102A (56-1216) of the 525th FIS during a visit to Soesterberg Air Base, The Netherlands, on 17 August 1965. The aircraft carries a White dart design painted on the drop tanks. (W. Snel)

This F-102A (56-1105) of the 525th FIS has the tips of the underwing fuel tanks in Red and is carrying an Air Force Outstanding Unit Award ribbon on the fin under the serial numner. The insignia on the fin band is the 86th Air Division badge. (Author)

The U.S. AIR FORCE legend on this F-102A (56-1044) of the 525th FIS has been painted in the wrong location; it should be further forward on the fuselage side. The aircraft has commander's stripes around the fuselage just behind the cockpit. (Author)

This F-102A (56-1131) of the 525th FIS has a White dart shaped design painted on the underwing drop tanks. The aircraft also carries an Outstanding Unit Award ribbon on the fin below the serial number. (A.G. v.d. Brink)

This F-102A (56-1077) of the 525th Fighter Interceptor Squadron carries an Air Force Outstanding Unit Award ribbon painted on the fin under the aircraft serial number. (Author)

A camouflaged F-102A (56-1105) of the 525th FIS on the ramp at Spangdahlem Air Base, Germany, on 20 May 1967. The Delta Dagger units often deployed to other NATO bases for training and exercises. (Author)

With its drag 'chute fully deployed, an F-102A pilot of the 525th FIS holds the nose off the runway for as long as possible to take full advantage of aerodynamic braking to shorten his landing rollout. (Author)

A camouflaged TF-102A (56-2331) of the 525th FIS taxies out during a
visit to Soesterberg Air Base, The Netherlands, on 3 May 1968. By the
late 1960s, most F-102s were in the Southeast Asia camouflage scheme.
(Author)

A line up of F-102As of the 525th FIS on the ramp at Bitburg Air Base,
Germany, during April of 1967. These Delta Daggers all carry the Southeast Asia camouflage scheme.

This F-102A (56-1237) of the 526th FIS was flown by the squadron commanding officer, LCOL R.J. Rankin, during 1962. The aircraft carried commander's stripes and his name on the nose in Black. (USAF via A. Pelletier)

526th Fighter Interceptor Squadron

The 526th Fighter Interceptor Squadron began conversion training of squadron pilots at Ramstein Air Base, Germany, on 1 August 1960. By November of that year, twenty-nine pilots had completed transition training in the F-102. To help maintain proficiency, an F-102 flight simulator was installed during January of 1960.

The first delivery of F-102s took place on 7 June 1960 when a flight of three F-102As were delivered from Saint-Nazaire, France. Over the next six months a total of twenty-nine F-102s were flown in, with the last two arriving on 2 December 1960.

By early October all the squadron's pilots had completed transition training and the unit began full scale combat crew training. At this point weather problems began to develop as the central European winter weather pattern set in. On top of that, the base commander announced that the runway would close for repairs. In order to meet their training requirements, the squadron requested and received authorization for a large scale deployment to Spain.

From 28 September until 17 October 1960, fourteen aircraft were deployed to Torrejon Air Base, Spain. The unit's TF-102A (54-1364)

was sent to Wheelus Air Base. The squadron's run of hard luck continued and normally sunny Torrejon suffered some of the worse weather it had seen all year, with high winds, thunderstorms and heavy rain showers. During the second week the weather improved and the 526th flew 120 sorties. As a result, the deployment was a complete success. On 15 November 1960 the 526th FIS assumed alert status with the F-102.

The unit made a number of deployments to Wheelus Air Base for weapons training. From 20 August to 1 September 1961 two flights of six aircraft each deployed and during August of 1962 a number of aircraft were once again deployed to Wheelus where they set a record of eleven hits of eleven missiles fired on a single day.

From 14 February 1963 to 1 June 1964 two JEF-102As of the AFSC were assigned to the 526th FIS to assist in the conversion of the GCI sites from the manual plotting and tracking equipment to the 412-L semi-automatic Air Weapons Control System. The two aircraft were administratively assigned to the 526th for maintenance and operational control.

The 526th FIS set a USAFE flight hours record during 1963. Their total of 7,400 hours was much higher than any other European F-102 squadron. During July, August and September of 1963, the squadron logged 1,976 hours, a ninety-day record for USAFE F-102 units. Flying time is allocated to an Air Division in much the same as its yearly budget of operating money. The time is then divided up

This TF-102A (54-1366) of the 526th FIS has a Red braking parachute housing and Red F-102 silhouettes on the nose. The aircraft was at Soesterberg Air Base on temporary assignment with the 32nd FIS during August of 1962 (Author)

The fin colors of this F-102A (56-1210) of the 526th FIS on the ramp at Ramstein Air Base, Germany, on 30 October 1963, were Red and White while the braking parachute housing was Red. (USAF)

among Division's squadrons. If a unit meets or exceeds its allowed flying time, it may be given flying time from other units that have been unable to meet their commitments because of weather, maintenance problems or other operational factors.

For their flight hours record, the 526th was named honor squadron of the 86th Air Division by the Division Commander BGEN F.W. Gillespie. This period of recognition extended from July to December of 1963. During April, May and June of 1964, the 526th set yet another record, flying 2,009 hours.

In late March 1964, CAPT Richard Carter distinguished himself by expertly handling a disabled F-102A. Just as he was taking off, CAPT Carter realized that the F-102 had blown a tire. Continued his climb he left the landing gear extended and had his wingman check for damage. Once the blown tire was confirmed, CAPT Carter circled the field burning down some 6,000 pounds of fuel to lower the aircraft's landing weight.

Once down to the proper weight, he lowered his field arrestor hook and engaged the BAK-9 barrier cable at the approach end of

the runway. For the landing, Carter was awarded the USAFE "Well Done" Award.

During October of 1964, CAPT Charles Monahan of the 526th received a USAFE "Well Done" Award for a safe landing in an almost uncontrollable F-102A. The aircraft had the throttle linkage fail in flight. CAPT Monahan manipulated the linkage with a pencil and his finger tips, while guiding another aircraft down — the second aircraft had experienced radio failure and was following Monahan down on the GCA approach. The pilot of the second F-102 was never aware of the throttle problem experienced by Monahan.

During April of 1965 the 526th made training deployments to two other NATO bases. Six F-102s were flown to Erding Air Base near Munich early in the month. Six other Delta Daggers were deployed at the end of April to Creil Air Base in France.

Probably the greatest operational hazard faced by F-102 units in the central European area was the weather and historical reports showed that Ramstein AB had the worse weather, in terms of ceilings

An F-102A (56-1214) of the 526th FIS on the ramp outside the alert hangar at Ramstein Air Base, Germany, on 30 October 1963. The only markings on the aircraft were the Red and White fin sunburst. (USAF)

An F-102A (56-1163) of the 526th FIS during a visit to Soesterberg Air Base, The Netherlands, on 30 October 1963. The crew name silhouettes on the nose were a common feature on USAFE F-102s during this time period.

and visibility, than any other base. As a result, the 526th routinely deployed aircraft to Spain during the winter months with deployments being made during February 1966, December 1966 and January 1967.

Competitions and Awards

To keep the pilots combat ready and to select the squadron's flight and pilot of the month, the 526th FIS initiated a monthly competition. The day-long tournament began with the participating crews receiving their briefing, special instructions and flight plans in the squadron crew briefing room. Each participating flight had selected four pilots for the competition.

The objective of the exercise was to determine how quickly each competing flight completed a successful intercept of a "target" aircraft. The "target" was another F-102 from the squadron, usually flown by the squadron commander COL H.B. Graham. After the "target" was positioned, a scramble was sounded over the unit "bullhorn." The pilots ran to there fighters and were airborne in a matter of minutes. The target flew at a predetermined altitude, usually 45,000 feet. Once airborne, the interceptors searched out the target with their radar and set up a climbing intercept starting at 40,000 feet. The F-102s climbed up to the target to complete the intercept

The intercept was recorded electronically on magnetic tape which was played back to the judges on the ground to determine if the interceptors had scored a kill. If the pilot kept the target within the missile release circle on his radar screen for two seconds, he scored three points for the intercept. During June of 1966 B flight won the competition.

During April of 1965 the Directorate of Aerospace Safety at Norton AFB, California, announced the selection of 526th FIS for a flying safety award. The squadron was honored for a total of 15,002 accident-free hours (compiled over a two year period).

The squadron's missile loading teams participated in the USAFE/LOADEO Competitions from 1965 until 1969. They won the competition in July of 1967, placing first in the F-102 category and also won as the overall competition winner with the highest total team points (5.037 out of a possible 6.000). In the NATO/AFCENT Air Defense Competition the squadron participated as part of a team made up of pilots from the 496th, 525th and 526th Fighter Interceptor Squadrons. They represented Sector 3 during September of 1965 and again in June of 1966 and May of 1969.

During 1967 the 526th FIS received the 86th Air Division's Outstanding Unit Award for the period January to March 1967.

Four pilots of the 526th marked a milestone in their careers during March of 1969 when each reached 1,000 flying hours in the Delta Dagger. These pilots were MAJs George D. Navarre and Richard H. Dunwoody, and CAPTs Lawrence C. Denson and John E. Peterson.

This JEF-102A (57-0836) was assigned to the 526th FIS for more than a year as part of a test program. The aircraft carried a Red fin tip with White stars and a Red triangle on the nose.

The tail band on this TF-102A (55-4059) of the 526th FIS was Red with a thin White outline. The insignia on the band is the 86th Air Division patch. The aircraft was departing Soesterberg Air Base after a stopover on 19 July 1966. (Author)

Colors

The F-102s of the 526th flew without markings of any kind from the time the Delta daggers were first delivered until early 1961 when the unit began applying the 86th Air Division sunburst fin markings. The unit also began using crew name Delta Dagger silhouettes on the nose during this time. During 1962, aircraft 56-1237 was painted as the unit commander's aircraft with a band consisting of four Red and three White stripes running around the fuselage just behind the cockpit. The braking parachute housing was sometimes painted in flight colors, Blue, Red or White.

During the autumn of 1963, the Red-White-Red-White sunburst fin markings were removed being replaced by plain Gray fins with the squadron insignia being carried on port side and the 86th AD insignia on the starboard side. The 526th had a number of aircraft painted with commander's stripes, probably because the squadron played host to six high ranking pilots from higher headquarters who maintained their F-102 proficiency by using 526th aircraft. These aircraft usually carried Red-White-Red stripes around the fuselage behind the cockpit.

During Autumn of 1964, the squadron applied a Red horizontal band on the fin with the squadron/86th AD insignias carried on the band. The band remained in use until at least until August of 1966.

The first camouflaged F-102s entered service at Ramstein on 8 November 1965. The last USAFE Dagger to be painted in the camouflage scheme was a 52nd TF-102A (54-1367) which returned from CASA on 5 July 1968.

Aircraft Accidents

The 526th suffered their share of accidents and incidents. On 6 January 1961, an F-102 (56-1239) of the 526th FIS crashed five miles short of the runway of Toul-Rossieres AB, France. Another F-102A (56-1235) was lost near Illesheim Army Airfield, Germany, on 5 March 1963.

After an engine explosion and fire, the unit's TF-102A (55-4059) crashed at Ramstein on 8 June 1967. The aircraft had been on a visit at Hahn Air Base and made a routine departure. At 12,000 feet a severe explosion occurred and the warning lights in the cockpit came on for the AC/DC generator and boost pumps. A short time later the fire warning light came on with a steady glow. Faced with a possible explosion, the pilots decided to eject. The Deuce continued a slow roll into a split-S and crashed at the airfield in a near vertical dive.

This F-102A (56-1202) of the 526th FIS had a White braking parachute housing and air intake splitter plate. The aircraft also has a Red F-102 silhouette on the underwing drop tank. (W. Snel)

An F-102A (56-1208) of the 526th FIS taxies in during a deployment to Soesterberg Air Base during 1965. The aircraft has a Blue drag 'chute housing and Red and White commander's stripes on the fuselage.

Two other aircraft were lost including 56-1234 which crashed on 5 March 1968. The aircraft struck a house about a mile southeast of Bobesheim, Germany; the pilot parachuted to safety. On 14 July 1969, another F-102A (56-1237) crashed thirty-five miles from Sembach AB, near the village of Ingweiler, France. The aircraft was part of a flight of three and had collided with his wingman (56-1263). Luckily the second F-102 was only slightly damaged.

Due to a faulty latch system, the unit's TF-102A (54-1364) lost its canopy during flight on 9 January 1964. At that time there was only one spare TF-102A canopy available in the entire Air Force. Unfortunately, it was in a PACAF squadron. The 526th was determined to have a higher priority for the canopy, so it was sent back from PACAF to Germany, taking some two months to arrive. On 20 October 1965 another F-102A (56-1242) was involved in a ground accident at Ramstein.

Phase Out

The last operational mission of a USAFE F-102 was made on 1 April 1970 by a flight of four Delta Daggers of the 526th FIS. The aircraft were piloted by MAJs Lelon Rousey and Hugh Davis along with CAPTs Kurt Anderson and Richard McGlumphy. These four pilots had compiled a total of more than 3,200 hours in the F-102 between them.

The first group of F-102s left Ramstein Air Base on 15 April 1970, followed by a second group of fourteen F-102s on 16 April 1970. These flights ended the service of the Convair F-102 Delta Dagger in USAFE. Other Delta Daggers were seen in Europe; however, these aircraft were visitors belonging to the 57th Fighter Interceptor Squadron, an Air Defense Command unit based at Keflavik, Iceland.

The 526th FIS was redesignated as a Tactical Fighter Squadron on 1 April 1970.

A power cart is hooked up to this F-102A (56-1234) of the 526th FIS on the ramp at Ramstein Air Base, Germany, during August of 1965. The aircraft carries a thin Red commander's stripe on the fuselage. (S. Peltz)

A 526th FIS F-102A (56-1237) on the taxiway at Soesterberg Air Base, The Netherlands, on 6 August 1965 during a cross country navigation flight. The aircraft carries three Red commander's stripes on the fuselage. (Author)

This F-102A (56-1249) of the 526th FIS has two F-102 silhouettes on the nosewheel door. The unit insignia is painted on the fin band and the braking parachute housing is in White.

An F-102A (56-1242) of the 526th Fighter Interceptor Squadron taxies in with the canopy raised during August of 1965. The cockpit of the F-102 could become very uncomfortable during the hot summer months with the canopy closed. (Author)

The barrel on the wooden stand next to this F-102A (56-1258) of the 526th FIS at Ramstein Air Base, Germany, during September of 1965 appears to be a weapons clearing barrel for line security personnel. (S. Peltz

The braking parachute housing is open indicating that the parachute has been deployed and cut loose on the taxiway for pickup by ground crews. This F-102A Delta Dagger was assigned to the 526th FIS during 1966. (Author)

A tow bar is hooked up to the nosewheel of this F-102A (56-1255) of the 526th FIS on the ramp at Ramstein, Germany, during September of 1965. The aircraft has two F-102 silhouettes painted on the nosewheel door. (S. Peltz)

This F-102A (56-0985) of the 32nd FIS on the taxiway at Soesterberg during August of 1963 has a Red, White and Blue braking parachute housing and a Red stripe on the air intake splitter plate. (Author)

Return to the United States

Two groups of F-102As and TF-102As returned to the U.S. during April and June of 1964 under Operation KRAZY KAT. On 15 April 1964, the first group left Ramstein Air Base, Germany, bound for Prestwick, Scotland. A second group left Hahn Air Base on 1 June 1964 also staging through Prestwick.

Detachment 6 of the 4440th Aircraft Delivery Group, based at Chateauroux Air Base, France, had overall responsibility for the move. MAJ. Isadore T. Porowski and CAPT Benjamin W. Van Wagner arranged support procedures in Germany and along the flight route. They also coordinated details pertaining to air rescue, weather and traffic control. Pilots for the operation were drawn from each of the six USAFE F-102 units and from several Delta Dagger units in the United States.

The following aircraft were involved in Operation KRAZY KAT:

15 April Aircraft Serial/ Squadron	1 June Aircrat Serial/Squadron
53411/32nd FIS	31807/496th FIS
53427/431st FIS	31810/496th FIS
53431/431st FIS	31816/496th FIS
53432/431st FIS	41376/496th FIS
53433/431st FIS	41385/496th FIS
53434/431st FIS	41389/496th FIS
53436/431st FIS	41393/496th FIS
53449/431st FIS	41395/496th FIS
53450/431st FIS	41397/496th FIS
53451/431st FIS	41399/496th FIS
53460/431st FIS	41406/496th FIS
31801/496th FIS	41407/496th FIS
31809/496th FIS	53393/496th FIS
31811/496th FIS	53418/32nd FIS
41392/496th FIS	53437/496th FIS
41394/496th FIS	53438/32nd FIS
41400/496th FIS	53448/431st FIS
41402/496th FIS	53456/32nd FIS
41405/496th FIS	41365/32nd FIS
41365/32nd FIS	53464/431st FIS
41367/431st FIS	70836/526th FIS
54034/497th FIS	70845/526th FIS
54041/497th FIS	

Project HARDWAY I and II

A further group of aircraft left Europe for delivery back to the U.S. during September and December of 1964:

22 September	2 December
53444/32nd FIS	60975/32nd FIS
53445/32nd FIS	60985/32nd FIS
53447/32nd FIS	60993/32nd FIS
53454/32nd FIS	60996/32nd FIS
61006/32nd FIS	61048/496th FIS
41364/526th FIS	
61247/526th FIS	

F-102A-50-Co (55-3447) 431st FIS, somewhere over the Libyan desert during July 1962. (S. Chianese)

After their return from Europe, a number of F-102As were reconditioned and issued to Air National Guard Squadrons throughout the U.S. These Delta Daggers are assigned to the Air National Guard (Larry Davis)

A number of F-102s were returned from Europe and saw service with various Air National Guard units. This camouflaged F-102A carries the Blue fin marking of the New York Air National Guard. (Larry Davis.)

After years of faithful service both in Europe and with the New York Air National Guard, these two F-102As were finally retired and placed in storage at Davis Monthon Air Force Base. (Larry Davis)

A flight of four camouflaged F-102As (56-0983, 56-1002, 56-1245 and 56-1014) of the 32nd Fighter Interceptor Squadron fly over The Netherlands during the late 1960s. The camouflage pattern was the same at that used on F-102s in Southeast Asia. (Sectie Militaire Luchtvaart Historie, RNethAF)

Camouflage

Late in the career of the F-102 in Europe the aircraft were given a camouflage paint scheme. This camouglage was originally designed for use in Southeast Asia as a result of the Vietnam War. While it was very effective for aircraft operating at low levels, it was not effective for a high altitude interceptor like the F-102 because the dark colors make the Delta Daggers very noticable against a light sky or clouds.

The official colors specified by USAF Technical Order TO 1-1-4 were Tan (FS 20400), Medium Green (FS 34102) and Dark Green (FS 34078) on the uppersurfaces and Light Gray (FS 36622) on the undersurfaces. Additionally, the national insignia was reduced in size and the large U.S. Air Force and USAF legends were deleted.

Most units operated a mix of ADC Gray and camouflaged F-102s during their phase out periods, with many of the camouflaged aircraft ending up with Air National Guard units in various states after they returned to the U.S. The camouflage period marked the beginning of the end for the F-102 Delta Dagger in Europe.

A camouflaged F-102A of the 32nd FIS on landing approach to Soesterberg Air Base, The Netherlands, on 10 April 1969. (Author)

A camouflaged F-102A-55-CO of the 32nd Fighter Interceptor Squadron lands at Soesterberg Air Base on 3 July 1968 with the braking parachute fully deployed. (Dave Menhard)

The trailing edge flaps on this camouflaged F-102A (56-1210) of the 526th FIS are drooping as the hydraulic pressure is bled off. By May of 1967, the career of the F-102 in Europe was coming to a close. (Author)

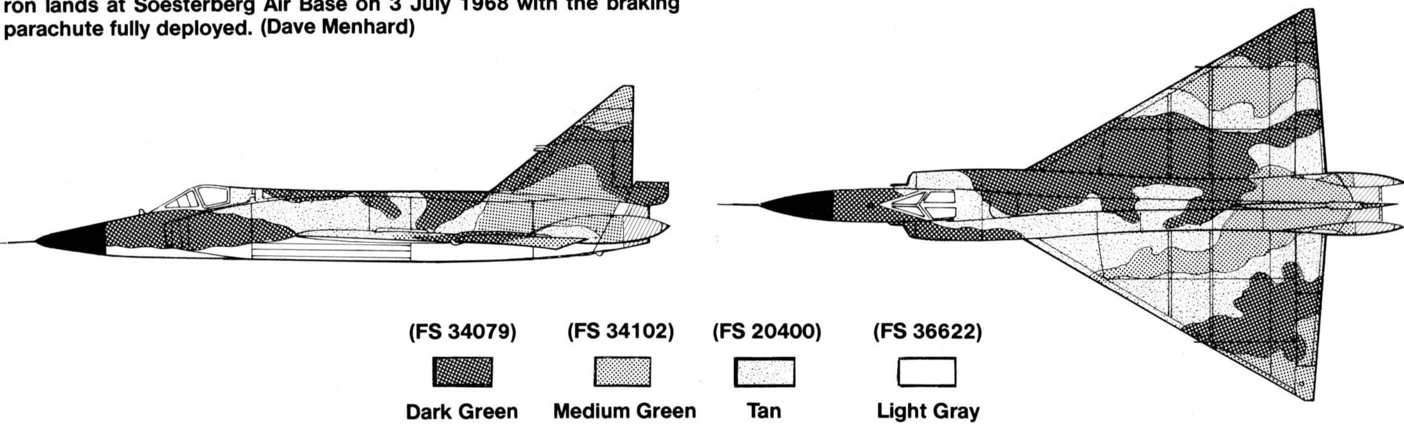